The
ESSENTIAL
GUIDE
to the
SHORT
TERM
MISSION
TRIP

David C. Forward

MOODY PRESS
CHICAGO

To my parents, Cedric and Leila Forward,
who instilled in me the importance of regular worship
and attendance in church,
which in our case was the local Salvation Army corps
in our small English village.

Thank you, Mum and Dad,
for putting me on the right track,
and fighting to keep me there.

And to Tony Campolo, whose words drew me back
into the family of Christ after a fifteen-year hiatus.
His sense of humor, his amazing ability to bring the Gospel home
with simple, memorable anecdotes, and the fact he lives his faith
out in the open every day make him a model for our times.

Thank you, Tony, for your simple eloquence
and your commitment to the fight for the cause of missions
and the Gospel of Jesus Christ.

CONTENTS

ACKNOWLEDGMENTS

The first two people I thank for helping make this book possible are two pastors: Richard A. Carter of Faith Presbyterian Church, in Medford, New Jersey (my home church), and Steven P. Moyer of Felton Presbyterian Church in Felton, California. Rick and Steve have enthusiastically supported every aspect of our mission work—even the "crazy" ideas. Both were of inestimable assistance in my preparation of this book, particularly in clarifying some of my grass roots theology. Rick is my most valued counselor and teacher, and I am proud and honored to him my pastor.

I also thank my dear wife and mentor, Chris, for her omnipresent encouragement and support, and Phil Warren for his wisdom and suggestions. I am grateful to my editor at Moody Press, Jim Vincent, for his professional and spiritual insights. Special thanks go to Julie Angove for her translation into Spanish of the Appendices, to Debbie Long for the French, and Adrian Ciorna for the Romanian versions.

I also thank mission professionals with several agencies, notably David Minich, John Yeatman, and Adrian Ciorna of Habitat for Humanity; Bruce Main of Urban Promise; representatives at Global Missions Fellowship; and Brian Sellers-Petersen at World Vision.

INTRODUCTION

*C*hristians are now living at one of history's great turning points. From a purely historical standpoint, we are about to enter the third millennium, an occasion that should cause all of us to take stock of what we have done to improve our world in the two thousand years since Christ walked among our ancestors.

Progress continues in resolving the material and spiritual needs of the world's inhabitants. During the past half century people have become more aware than in all the preceding nineteen of the need to conserve our planet's resources. We realize that fresh water, arable land, and food are actually available in plentiful supply in much of North America and portions of Europe. The need remains for those of us who are blessed with an abundance of those commodities to share them with our human brothers and sisters whose geographic access to them is limited. We must not waste but rather distribute our bounty.

Spiritual needs also are great. The good news of spiritual deliverance through Jesus Christ remains an equally important resource that Christians must share. As we enter the twenty-first century, we have greater capabilities to do so. Christians are better educated, more globally conscious, and more technically equipped to take the Gospel to unchurched and unreached people groups than ever before.

As we declare the Gospel to those who have not yet heard, we must recognize that a massive shift has occurred in the way Christians take the Word into the world. For hundreds of years, it

has been left to ordained career missionaries to leave their homeland for distant shores, determined to take Christianity to the
heathen masses. Undeniably, that method has worked, and we
owe a huge debt to the many brave, committed missionaries who
gave their lives to fulfill the Great Commission which Jesus issued
to us all. During the past generation, however, a movement has
gained momentum to aid long-term mission enterprises with
short-term mission projects, using Christian workers whose skills,
while not available year after year, can supplement the spiritual
and natural gifts of career missionaries (and local church leaders). These short-term missionaries have become an effective
army for Christ.

It is for these short-term missionaries and their team leaders
that this book is written. Team leaders, whether ordained or from
the laity, will benefit from its advice on how to build, plan, and
lead a group of people with differing interests and objectives,
molding them into one team with the singular purpose of building the kingdom of God as servant disciples. But it is also for the
participant in that team. It will help the short-term mission worker to focus on why he or she is going and offer practical tips on
how to make the trip more fulfilling. In addition, the participant
will receive suggestions from hundreds of previous short-termers
on how to make a difference in the host community.

No Christian can choose to disregard missions. As we will
see, missions have been a central element of God's law from the
earliest recorded prophets to the last book of the New Testament.
Jesus Himself chose to spend His precious last hours on earth
commanding us to "Go into all of the world" with His message before the Ascension. When we accepted Jesus Christ as our personal Savior, we issued a promissory note to Him. We agreed to
follow His decrees in our daily walk for the rest of our lives. Knowing that we can never rise to the standards He set Himself, we nevertheless cannot abdicate our responsibility to try, in the way we
treat others, the way we maintain our own conduct, and the way
we spread the Good News throughout the world.

Yet believers now see a paradigm shift in the way they best accomplish that work—a shift that has largely taken place in just the
last two or three decades. The increasing use of short-term workers is one of several aspects of this new paradigm. The new mod-

els for the mission enterprise offer a fresh perspective, including:

- A shift in how we view ourselves. Increasingly we see ourselves as "World Christians," recognizing that we are part of the global family of humankind. We do not have all the answers. We cannot assume the colonial position of going into developing nations to take "our" Gospel to the "illiterate natives." We should instead study their traditions and culture and try to understand and work with the people in our mission fields.

- Major changes in the role and image of the career missionaries. Movies and history books for centuries mislabeled the career missionary as "The Great White Hope"—of movies and history books. Today that tag is more erroneous than ever. Fewer long-term missionaries from the West serve today than anytime this century. Indeed, one positive evolution has been the fact that today hundreds of missionaries are sent from the very countries which received the Word from our own mission professionals a few years ago: Korea, Africa, the Philippines, are shining examples. Many nations no longer allow foreign missionaries to enter. Thus the work is now being done by local Christians. In India, for two centuries a destination popular with missionaries from Britain, there is phenomenal success being experienced by putting Indian nationals through the briefest of training and then sending them into communities where they have no language nor cultural gap. Bringing a thousand souls to Christ and starting a half-dozen churches is not unusual for each missionary—in just his first year!

- A shift in the way the Western churches are sending their missionaries. There are many more short-term mission workers than earlier this century. For the latter part of this century, many denominations have experienced a drop in financial support for mission work. Yet when they offered members of their congregations the opportunity to personally participate in short-term missions, tiny groups traversed the world for the cause. Members of

Southern Baptist churches alone sent more than 75,000 short-termers and 81,000 volunteers in missions in 1996. Such activities serve several purposes. They accomplish some tasks the smaller corps of career missionaries is unable to do. They imbue the short-termers with a sense of enthusiasm and self-fulfillment for missions overall that they then spread throughout their congregations when they return home. Through this reawakening of the vital need for missions—now seen through the faces and names and anecdotes of real people in the host communities—it reverses the decline in mission support overall. No small consolation has been the discovery by many short-term mission participants that they want to make missions a larger part of their lives, and they commit some of their post-college, or early retirement years to the call.

• A focus on people groups rather than entire nations. This recognizes that we cannot look at any one country and paint with one brush a picture of the culture and religion of all its citizens. Thus we find 600 people groups delineated in the USA and Canada alone, 1,550 people groups in Asia (excluding China, India, and Muslim countries), and 2,800 people groups in Africa. "Muslims," traditionally lumped together as one, no matter whether they lived in Morocco or Indonesia, are identified into 4,030 recognizable, distinct people groups today. Of course, this further complicates the work missionaries do, since we cannot now look at a nation where they have attained some successes and score it with a huge check mark.

The partnership between the sending church and the receiving one, between the on-site mission professional and the short-term mission team, between the western Christians and the new converts in the less-developed nation benefits everybody. The host community gets something they need accomplished by the team; the mission field representative need not spend her precious budget on something the incoming team will self fund; the sending church derives enormous benefits from a core of charged-up enthusiastic members who often go on to lead in other lay roles.

More important, we are fulfilling the will of our Lord Jesus Christ. We *are* taking His message into all the world, we *are* being good stewards of what He entrusted to us, and we *are* helping our brethren in need. What a great moment in history to share with one another. Let us rejoice and be glad in it: better yet, let us go out and do something about it!

Chapter One

WHAT ARE MISSIONS?
(AND WHY SHOULD WE CARE?)

J remember the meeting so well. Those of us who were involved in a mission project in Romania were gathering in Chicago for a weekend retreat. As my friend and I walked into the reception after a journey of several hours, an Iowa pastor greeted us.

"Aha!" he exclaimed, seeing our New Jersey towns on the name badges. "I see you are from the Liberal East!" Later, while he was speaking to the entire group, he described his church as "Bible based." For a while, his condescending attitude bothered me. *A Bible based church indeed,* I thought. *What did he think we based our church on, the tales of Brer Rabbit? After all, are not all Christian churches Bible based?*

The focus of this book is to discover how to create and operate successful mission trips. Like the well-meaning pastor who knew his church was Bible based, we need to be confident that our short-term missions trips are based on and follow the instructions in the Bible.

A DIFFERENT PURPOSE

I have been a proud member of a Rotary Club for twenty years. In that time, I have done everything I could to live the ideals of this fine service organization, dealing ethically with customers and employees, developing high moral standards among our youth, and giving my all in humanitarian service projects

both locally and around the world. However, there is a fundamental difference between humanitarian projects and mission
projects. The difference is the purpose. Only one is Bible based,
doing good works to honor Jesus Christ.

Compare a wonderful project where Rotarians from southern New Jersey built an orphanage in the Dominican Republic
with another where Christians built an orphanage in Beius, Romania. On the surface, both programs looked alike: they involved
personal sacrifice, the spirit of volunteerism, acts of great generosity, and many committed, hardworking people. The difference between the two projects was that the second was a Christian
endeavor, and as such, those participating answered to a higher
calling. They were not better people; they just responded to the
call of Christ as opposed to simply doing good works.

Notice the different motives of the two groups. The Rotari-
an team did their good work because they cared about their fellow man and wanted to make a difference. Those are noble,
commendable reasons. Yet the church missions team gave their
time and talents because they were inspired by the Scriptures to
be disciples and do the work in the name of Jesus Christ, their
personal Lord and Savior.

We know many people have great needs. Our response can
address their physical needs *and* their spiritual needs. Not all service projects do that, of course. For instance, suppose a builder
forms a group of compassionate, generous tradesmen called
"Contractors Who Care." They go to Haiti to build an AIDS clinic
in response to the physical need. They believed it was necessary,
felt good doing the work, and the Haitians certainly appreciated
it. The volunteers worked on the project from sunup until dark.
They ate, collapsed into bed, only to repeat it all again the next
day. During their work trip they barely met any local people, and
did not share their faith with them. They saw their mandate as
building the clinic, and that is exactly what they did. They did not
see their mandate as addressing the spiritual needs of the community they served.

In contrast, there are Christian groups that give far less attention to the physical needs. When some church outreach groups
became involved in a ministry called Trevor's Campaign for the
Homeless, some Christians believed they should not give out

food and blankets to the folks sleeping on Philadelphia's mean streets until the Gospel was preached to them. In fact, if the street teams had preached and not even had any food or blankets, some people back in the home churches would not have seen that as a problem. They would have addressed the spiritual needs (as the critics saw them) to the exclusion of all other demands.

Meanwhile, in Zaire, half a world away, one missionary says simply, "An empty stomach has no ears." One cannot evangelize a hungry person and ignore his physical needs. Which approach is correct?

BALANCING PHYSICAL AND SPIRITUAL NEEDS

The answer seems to be balance: Christians need to address both physical and spiritual needs. Let us address the physical hunger, homelessness, disease, etc., and as those helped have strength and curiosity, tell them *why* we are helping.

When we arrange mission work teams, some members love to build new churches, while others help to construct orphanages and Christian clinics. Some people spend every moment they can tending to abandoned babies and orphaned children. Yet other team members are chomping at the bit to get out and evangelize. One group found out the day after their eighteen-hour journey that they could preach that very day in several villages. They were thrilled, and by sunset that Sunday the three lay preachers had delivered nine sermons in eight different villages.

As team leaders, we can teach each member of a team to be prepared to personally address both spiritual and physical needs. They often will appear hesitant to share their faith at first, but by the time your team leaves, they can be ready. And opportunities will come. Without fail, groups I've been in, while delivering food to a remote mountain village, will meet someone who describes their plight and is comforted when that once-scared team member says, "Would you like me to pray with you?"

A. Leonard Tuggy, former overseas foreign secretary to Asia for the Conservative Baptist Foreign Missions Society, wrote:

> Though the word *mission* is related to the work of the church, missions (with the *s*) is rich in its associations. Missions include all the things missionaries do—evangelizing, discipling, teaching, heal-

ing, administering, writing and preaching. In missions all these activities are done in conscious obedience to the Great Commission. This has been the meaning of missions for at least two hundred years.[1]

Tuggy explained that we cannot trace the plural *missions* to the New Testament. Its current meaning thus has to be determined from the way Christians have used it through the years. "'As the Father has sent me, so I send you,' Jesus said in John 20:21 [NRSV]. Jesus was sent into the world to perform a definite mission. And so are we."

In *Presbyterians in World Mission,* author G. Thompson Brown has defined the word *mission* this way:

> The verb "send" is the clue to our understanding of God's mission in the world. For behind the English word "mission" is the Latin *missus*—to send. The original meaning is preserved in our word "missile." The church "in mission" is God's missile or projectile which is hurled into the world! Behind the Latin word *missus* is the Greek *apostolos.* The apostles were the "sent ones" —sent out by Jesus into the world even as the Father had sent Him. "Mission," then, is the church in motion, the activity of the church as it is sent into the world. Mission must include evangelism and social action, church planting and Christian education, compassion and justice. Its concern is with the individual and society. But at its center is the witness to the Good News—by word and deed. Without the word, the witness is unintelligible. Without the deed the witness has no credibility.[2]

Centuries earlier, St. Francis of Assisi must have been thinking along similar lines when he wrote, "Preach the Gospel . . . and if necessary, use words."

THE FOUR THEMES OF MISSIONS

Just as my thoughts from that Chicago retreat were "Are not all churches Bible based?" so the fundamental basis for this book is that all mission work is based on the clear instructions given us in the Bible. We can categorize our mandate for mission work in four themes, not ranked here in order of importance: (1) the oneness of humankind; (2) our covenant relationships; (3) our role as servant disciples of Jesus Christ; and (4) our commission as evangelists. Let's consider the importance of each.

1. The Oneness of Humankind

Sometimes it seems our human race is anything but unified. We see and judge each other too often by race, religion, or socioeconomic class, frequently building barriers where we should be celebrating common bonds. It can be downright disheartening to have church members disparage a mission project to the inner city in barely suppressed racial tones, or a program to help the homeless dismissed with such comments as, "Let them get a job." Even people of faith describe others as "fundamentalist," "evangelical," or "liberal," using the labels as derogatory tags, rather than as brothers and sisters created in the true image of God.

" 'For you have only one Master, and you are all brothers,' " Jesus told His disciples and the crowds that followed Him (Matthew 23:8). Later the apostle Paul admonished Christians to "Live in harmony with one another. Do not be proud, but be willing to associate with people of low position" (Romans 12:16). His wish and hope for the Christians was for unity: "May the God who gives endurance and encouragement give you a spirit of unity among yourselves as you follow Christ Jesus. . . . Accept one another, then, just as Christ accepted you, in order to bring praise to God" (Romans 15:5, 7). Another apostle, Peter, wrote, "Finally, all of you, live in harmony with one another; be sympathetic, love as brothers, be compassionate and humble" (1 Peter 3:8).

These excerpts should have all Christians nodding in complete agreement. Unity in spirit and purpose is a basic tenet of our faith and of human decency. Sadly, there is much disagreement within the body of Christ. The scope of this book cannot address the tensions among Christians and toward some groups of unbelievers. However, many problems are self-induced because we were not aware of the cultural differences among different social and ethnic groups—both differences among Christians and between Christians and nonbelievers. (In a later chapter, we will look at some examples of disunity among mission team members.)

As a missions group member or leader, you should expect such disunity. Start a mission program that helps pregnant teens, minority youth, or the needy in some faraway land and you should be prepared for people whom you held in the highest esteem to challenge your deeds. You will learn that the old maxim of never pleasing everyone must have first been coined by someone who tried something new in a church!

Yet the first chapter of Genesis confirms that we are one race, created by God and sharing the same ancestry: "Then God said, 'Let us make man in our image, in our likeness'" (Genesis 1:26). So the Bible tells us that we are to live together, sharing our love, encouragement, and compassion, especially with those of low position, because all human beings are created in the image of God.

2. Living a Covenant Relationship

As Christians, we take our covenants, or solemn vows, seriously. We had better, for there is a long trail of broken lives of those who make, and foolishly break, their promises. Yet the Lord is steadfast and gives us the promise of life everlasting because of His unwavering covenants with us.

On the night before Christ died, He ate the Last Supper with His disciples when He introduced the New Covenant. The writer of the book of Hebrews explained, "By calling this covenant 'new,' he has made the first one obsolete" (Hebrews 8:13). Later the writer added that Christ Himself had shed His own blood to purify our own lives, "For this reason Christ is the mediator of a new covenant, that those who are called may receive the promised eternal inheritance" (Hebrews 9:15).

So what must we do to fulfill our side of the promise we have made with God, the covenant we agreed to the moment we accepted Jesus Christ as our personal Savior? In the Great Commission, Jesus told His followers, "'All authority in heaven and on earth has been given to me. Therefore go and make disciples of all nations, baptizing them in the name of the Father and of the Son and of the Holy Spirit'" (Matthew 28:18–20). What a simple, eloquent directive for each of us to follow in our daily lives, even two thousand years later.

Jesus loved telling simple stories. A case in point was the time He told how He was hungry and His disciples had refused to feed Him; tired, yet they withheld a bed; parched from thirst, yet they would not even give Him a drink of water. His shocked followers could barely hold in their hurt feelings as they protested, "Lord when did we ever see you [this way] and not help you?" To which He replied, "When you refused to help the least of these my brothers, you were refusing help to me" (See Matthew. 25:31–45 TLB).

Barbara Sawyer, who writes the "Deacon Diary" in my church's monthly newsletter, once explained in the column how Jesus is involved in our acts of kindness. "One of our Thanksgiving basket recipients wrote, 'Thank you for being Jesus to us'" she reported. "It's funny how Jesus is on both sides of the equation. Jesus is the giver, Jesus is the recipient. We give because He gave; we give to those He represents. He is the love in all of us, and the need in all of us."

Our part of the covenant relationship is to make disciples and to serve others as if we are serving Christ. These are the spiritual and physical aspects of missions work in action. Our covenant relationships with God and with our fellow human beings are clearer today than they have ever been. God tells us that if we follow Him with the faith and obedience of Abraham, we need not fear. We know through the New Covenant that Jesus Christ gave His own life so that our own sins will be forgiven. Our response to that should be to be faithful, obedient to God's law, and to treat every person we meet as if he were Christ Himself, while using every opportunity to share our faith and God's promises with the person.

That is our side of the covenant. In reality, of course, we know that on the day of reckoning God will have fulfilled *both* sides of the covenant: the human side will be fulfilled by the perfect obedience of Jesus, on behalf of those who trust in His saving work.

3. Our Lives as Servant Disciples of Jesus Christ

"O Lord, truly I am your servant; I am your servant, the son of your maidservant; you have freed me from my chains. I will sacrifice a thank offering to you and call on the name of the Lord. I will fulfill my vows to the Lord in the presence of all his people, in the courts of the house of the Lord—in your midst, O Jerusalem. Praise the Lord" (Psalm 116:16–19).

The beautiful words of the psalmist serve as the great equalizer for modern-day Christians. They teach us to be humble before God, young or old, wealthy businesspeople or poor and unemployed. In one simple sentence the psalmist reminds us of the freedom from the chains of worry and sin that comes when we place our lives at the feet of the Master.

Jesus Christ Himself repeated that truth when He invited His followers to "Come to me, all you who are weary and burdened, and I will give you rest. Take my yoke upon you and learn from me, for I am gentle and humble in heart, and you will find rest for your souls. For my yoke is easy and my burden is light" (Matthew 11:28–30). What comfort! What a promise! He is truly our Savior! In these words, Jesus is assuring us that He will answer our spiritual needs; no matter how troubled we are, no matter how deeply we have sinned nor how worrisome our crisis: If we go as servants to Christ in prayer and serve the Master and others humbly and sincerely, He will calm our fears.

One way the weary and burdened, the poor and the suffering can be delivered from their plight is through their faith and prayers. Yet what about their physical needs? That is where we come in: addressing the physical needs is the heart of mission work. "Carry each other's burdens," the Scripture commands (Galatians 6:2 KJV). Our own faith and loyalty to God's commandments open our eyes to see those needs and do something about them.

There is a caution here. When we decide to help our brothers and sisters in need, we must first adopt a servant attitude toward them. Jesus said as much:

> When he had finished washing their feet, he put on his clothes and returned to his place. "Do you understand what I have done for you?" he asked them. "You call me 'Teacher' and 'Lord,' and rightly so, for that is what I am. Now that I, your Lord and Teacher, have washed your feet, you also should wash one another's feet. I have set you an example that you should do as I have done for you." (John 13:12–15)

In the missions setting, servanthood does not mean that we must be helpless, irresolute, have no motivation, nor that we must be dependent on others for direction. We need only look at the original sent ones—the twelve apostles—to see how true servants act. The apostles surrendered their lives to God. They used every situation they encountered to serve Him: sharing the Gospel and ministering to the needy in Christ's name. Servanthood, then, means to do things for our Lord with the emphasis and motivation being not our own self-satisfaction nor personal ambition (or even how good such deeds might look on a college or job application) but for the glory of God and His grace.

In a story he has told before many audiences, author and sociology professor Tony Campolo describes the right and wrong way to deliver food baskets to the poor, baskets that so many churches prepare at holiday times. The worst way, Campolo says, is to knock on the door and say, "Hello, I'm from First Church. We would like to give you this food basket." Such an act, while founded on a generous idea, makes the giver feel good and the recipient feel humbled, dependent, and embarrassed. Instead, to give a poor family a food basket, sneak up to the house after dark, quietly leaving it on the doorstep. Then, Campolo says, "Call them from a nearby phone. When the family answers, say, 'One of God's servants who loves you has left something for you on the front step,' and then hang up."

Some participants on humanitarian projects and mission teams spend much of their own money to go along, only to gripe incessantly when they get there. They moan about the cold showers, they protest that the locals have body odor, they complain that the van taking relief supplies to impoverished villagers has no air conditioning. In short, they just don't get it!

As servants, we should have two attitudes. First, we need to lie down before God, pledging our service to Him as the humblest, least worthy of His servants. That is the attitude in Psalm 116:16. Second, we should regard ourselves as servants toward those we meet in mission outreach. That can be far tougher. Remember the passage where the disciples denied they would ever refuse help to their Lord (Matthew 25:31–45). I suspect most of us feel the same way. Yet when we come across somebody in need who does not look liked the white-skinned, blue-eyed, bearded picture adorning so many of our churches, it is easy to turn away. It is hard to look at an inebriated homeless man sleeping on a heating vent and think of ourselves as being his servant.

How can we do that? We must always remember that it is

Christ who works through us—and we are merely the instruments used in His service.

That is where Matthew 25 helps. When we look at that person, we can imagine we are looking right through their eyes and can see Jesus Himself. After all, surely this is among the "least of these our brothers." Then it is easy to say to yourself, "Here is food, here is water. Take, eat. For as I do this for my brother, so I am doing it for You, Lord." When we do those things willingly and humbly we demonstrate God's love in action.

After all, who are we not to act this way when "the Son of Man came not to be served but to serve, and to give his life a ransom for many" (Matthew 20:28 NRSV)?

4. Our Commission as Evangelists

William Carey, the father of modern missions, published his five Clear Convictions back in 1792 as he established the first missionary society in India:

1. The Great Commission is binding for every generation.
2. The growth of Christianity in history confirms this affirmation.
3. The world needs the Gospel.
4. There are no real impediments to getting the task done.
5. New mission societies must be created in every denomination.

Can anyone dispute the worthiness of Carey's declaration today—more than two centuries after he wrote those words?

Certainly, he was right that "the world needs the Gospel." Many still await the Good News. Fully half the world's population now lives in communities or cultural groups without a Christian witness. Sociologists project that by the year 2000, that sad statistic will include the majority of our planet's 6.5 billion people. Even today, most people born in developing nations have no exposure to Jesus Christ.

Who can deny the importance of global missions when so many needs have not been met: the spiritual needs of the unchurched, the physical needs of the 500 million people who live on the edge of starvation, the 100 million children who live on the streets of the world's cities, and the one billion who suffer from disease? "Mission is not an optional activity that can be delegated to voluntary societies, special groups, or individual enthusiasts. *It is the business of the church*," Brown writes in *Presbyterians in World Missions*.

The very term *evangelism* sends fear into the minds of many members of mainline denominations. They would seemingly prefer a dip in hot oil than go out evangelizing! Yet without evangelism, the church will die. Think of our secular world for a moment. If the coaches of the championship sports team do not recruit new young players, the team will self-destruct in just a few years. If a firm fires the marketing department and no longer looks for new customers, how long will the business last? A pastor friend once told me, "The last working member of our congregation retired this week." Think of all those decent, upstanding church members who over the years have said under their breath, "Evangelism? Not me," and who are now looking at a small membership with few ministries and little vitality. Many churches with dwindling membership rolls have forgotten the duty and joy of winning lost souls. Though it may seem at times a challenge, evangelism is our solemn obligation. It is never "not my job."

Missions authority David M. Howard wrote:

> The missionary enterprise of the church is not a pyramid built upside down with its point on one isolated text in the New Testament out of which we have built a huge structure known as "missions." Rather, the missionary enterprise of the church is a great pyramid built right side up, with its base running from Genesis 1 to Revelation 22. All of Scripture forms the foundation for the outreach of the gospel to the whole world.[3]

The model that compels us to do evangelistic mission work today can be found in Matthew 9:35: "Jesus went through all the towns and villages, teaching in their synagogues, preaching the good news of the kingdom and healing every disease and sickness."

Members of mission teams need to prepare to evangelize. Since the main purpose of this chapter is to understand that mission work today is based on directives set out for us in God's

Word, let us reflect for a moment on the key passage describing the sending of two of the first missionaries, Paul and Barnabas. Other than Jesus Christ, was there ever a man who attracted more people to the early church than Paul? Yet the beginning of Paul's ministry seems so understated: "While they were worshiping the Lord and fasting, the Holy Spirit said, 'Set apart for me Barnabas and Saul [Paul] for the work to which I have called them.' So after they had fasted and prayed, they placed their hands on them and sent them off" (Acts 13:2–3).

Paul then traveled from town to town, crossing national borders, telling people in twos and threes and in large assemblies the Good News. He helped start churches wherever he went. During his many years in prison, instead of feeling sorry for himself, he continued to evangelize, writing letters of hope and encouragement to the new believers. Look at the results of Paul's mission work—despite his spending much of his adult life in jail. Now consider the results we could realize without such restrictions.

Today's mission team members need not copy Paul's total sacrifice to qualify as evangelists. Nevertheless, they need to recognize and accept their responsibilities and duties. People in their destination will look at them, wondering who they are and why they are there. Thus, the team members should *act* like disciples of Christ.

Evangelism comes in many ways. It is Billy Graham standing in a football stadium, preaching to 100,000 people. Yet it is also one person, quietly explaining to an adjacent airplane passenger how Christ became her personal Savior. It is a mission team, praying together in a crowded restaurant; it is also one member of the team who offers to pray with the elderly, lonely widow to whom he has just delivered food.

Many Christians find it easier to share their faith in a distant mission site than to do so at home. It is not difficult, but to feel completely comfortable, you should practice what you are going to say. Chapter 8 offers some suggestions on how to prepare for evangelism. Even if you feel nervous about the prospect, you will end up experiencing a new self-confidence and a closer relationship with God, after your preparations for sharing your faith are completed.

We started this chapter by discussing the difference between a service club's humanitarian project and a Christian mission trip. We can be grateful for the many kind, caring, generous Rotarians, Lions, Boy Scouts, and the like who do great acts of kindness in the world. But the motive is as important as the strategy. The good deeds of Christians, done in response to God's call, provide both physical and spiritual hope for the needy. Nelson Bell, the well-known missionary doctor said, "If you separate evangelism and social action, you have only delivered half a gospel."

As Christians, preparing for a mission work trip, we have a motive far beyond good deeds. We go to give a cup of cold water—and the Gospel—in the name of Jesus. We can be confident that we are fulfilling our part of the covenant described in the Bible. You will be helping humankind as humble servant disciples of Christ; doing so while proclaiming to observers that the reason is Jesus Christ Himself loved the world so much He died on the cross for us. What a wonderful basis for a mission trip!

NOTES

1. A. Leonard Tuggy, "Mission and Evangelism: Is There a Difference?," *Impact*, September 1977, 11.
2. G. Thompson Brown, *Presbyterians in World Missions* (Decatur, Ga.: CTS Press, 1988), 5.
3. David M. Howard, *The Great Commission for Today* (Downers Grove, Ill.: InterVarsity, 1976), 31.

Chapter Two

※

WHY RUN SHORT-TERM MISSION TRIPS?

*Y*ou may not ask the question, but some members of your church will: Why run short-term missions trips? If you are planning to be a member of a short-term missions team, you can expect a variation of that question: Why participate in a missions trip? Our first response to such questions must be, "Because our Lord Himself told us to do so." His clear instructions were to go into the world and tend to the spiritual and physical needs of the impoverished and poor in spirit. A short-term missions trip is a practical and quick way to do that. It also helps church members understand Christian missions better and even consider full-time missions service.

So why do so many local churches abdicate their responsibility to send out missionaries? How often have you heard a sermon that encouraged people to explore the call to serve in the mission field? Where is it written that the initiative to find and motivate those *sent ones* should emanate from denominational headquarters? Even today, with short-term missions becoming extraordinarily popular, many local churches—ordained leaders and their governing councils—are so wrapped up in day-to-day concerns that they treat missions as an afterthought—if they think of it at all.

In his book *On the Crest of the Wave*, Peter Wagner writes:

> Some things in life are optional and some are not.
> Wearing shoes is optional. But eating is not.
> Driving a car is optional. But once you choose the option, dri-
> ving on the right-hand side of the road (here in America) is not.
> Becoming a Christian is optional. But once you decide to ask Je-
> sus Christ to take control of your life, involvement in world mis-
> sions is no longer optional.
> I'm not saying that these things are impossible.
> You can choose to go without eating, but if you do, you must
> take the consequences. . . You can choose to drive on the left but
> you will pay fines and cause accidents.[1]

Significantly, people like helping people, and that makes service appealing to a would-be short-term missions worker. If you watched the news every day, it would be easy to come away with the feeling we live in a brutal, uncaring world. Yet the nightly news does not reflect our society. Dozens of companies have adopted policies that encourage their employees to serve community needs. Despite headlines of corporate greed, I found a spirit of service alive during interviews with company workers for my book on volunteerism, *Heroes after Hours*.

I remember interviewing Zanny Shealey, an IBM employee who lives his faith as he gives dozens of hours each month working one-on-one with kids in Atlanta's youth correction facility. Many of those "dead-end kids" whom society had written off, came out of prison, finished their education, and have gone straight ever since. General Electric's Cristina Harter initiated a tutoring program which has inspired thousands of "at-risk" children in Schenectady, New York, to turn Ds and Fs into As and Bs for the first time in their lives. Dan North, a Christian who always wanted to do missionary work, but could never afford to go on mission trips, now works for Boeing. He came up with the idea of filling Boeing's jetliners with relief supplies whenever they delivered a new aircraft to a country with urgent medical needs or famine. He may not have gone on a short-term mission trip, but now, every few days he watches as another huge jet lumbers aloft from Boeing Field, filled with tons of lifesaving supplies.[2]

A GREAT NEED, A GREAT JOY

It is hard for me to stop at three examples. My point is that every one of the "heroes" about whom I wrote so much of his or her time, talent, and treasure to people in need. Yet to listen to them excitedly tell of the joy they felt from giving, you quickly realize that the adage "It is better to give than to receive" is true. Come to think of it, maybe that is the view Christ has of us: He gave far more to us than He ever would get back. But now, as He sees our response—passing on His love when we humbly and freely share our time and faith with others—He must rejoice with gladness.

The practical reason for sending mission teams is that there is much work to be done. We cannot ignore those needs once Christ has made us aware of them and has blessed us with the ability to do the job. For any one of us, the task may be impossible, but as the saying goes, "Many hands make light work."

Earle Palmer, a respected American evangelist of the mid-twentieth century, used a bicycle wheel as the model for church missions. He noted that in the days of horse-drawn wagons, the cartwheels had four spokes. When one of the spokes pointed to the ground as the wheel turned, that spoke bore the entire weight of the cart all by itself. Consequently, a spoke and then the wheel would often break. But today's bicycle wheel is different. Each spoke is so thin a child can twist it in knots. But when combined with all the other "weak" spokes, the wheel becomes unbreakable. The many spokes, working together, equally distribute the weight of the bicycle and rider among all the spokes.

Palmer's analogy is apropos for any Christian work, whether a local homeless program or an irrigation project in a distant land. Instead of relying on the traditional weight-bearers (pastors, career missionaries), if we do the job as a team, the work will be completed faster, better, and with less stress on the participants.

THE REWARDS OF SERVICE

One of the top computer salespeople in America, Tom Stormer of Digital Computer, once told me, "Whenever you are presenting a product to a potential customer, they are subliminally asking themselves, 'What's in it for me?'" His point was that you should always describe your product or service in language the customer sees will benefit him. We have established the scriptural basis for missions, but we must recognize as well practical benefits: you and your team members will receive much from working on a short-term mission project.

Learning How to Serve

Experienced mission leaders recall example after heart-warming example of teams that go out as polite strangers, only to return a week or two later and hug each other in tears as they part. They have grown as human beings, and as Christians, from the mission experience. As missionary Dr. Albert Schweitzer said, "I don't know what your destiny will be, but one thing I do know, the ones among you who will be really happy are those who have sought and found how to serve."

What's in it for you? Daily you will learn how you can be a servant of God. My wife, Chris, has been a constant inspiration as well as an important partner in my own missions work. She once told me how grateful she was for the focus of a missions project. "When we are on a mission team, the first thing we think about is 'How can I be a useful servant of the Lord?' The last thing we ask Him before we close our eyes at night is, 'Was I able to make a difference today? Please empower me to do so tomorrow.'"

Working on a mission team rids us of our normal distractions, like a favorite TV program, work, or caring for a child. Those diversions are replaced by the focused determination on being a better Christian—yes, a servant disciple to the real needs we see around us at the mission site. Another team member described it as "Being a full-time Christian rather than just a Sunday-morning Christian."

That feeling of being what the Lord wants us to be is rewarding. He shows us that having commanded us to "Go and make disciples of all nations," He will not push us out of the nest on our own. He will be there the whole way as the wind beneath our wings.

One team member, Chuck, felt very nervous about publicly sharing his testimony. Then he did so in a tiny overseas village and as a result saw several people ask Christ to become their Savior. His joy was wondrous to behold! One young believer from strife-torn Belfast spent a summer working in Camden, New Jersey; his fervent faith persuaded one street gang member to forsake drugs and follow Jesus and inspired other team members.

One talented member of a short-term group in Hungary repaired an elderly lady's hearing aid. The Hungarian woman's face lit up as she heard for the first time in years, and the handy member considered his whole mission trip worthwhile.

Watching Miracles Take Place

And occasionally, members witness miracles during their missions adventures. Things happen that cannot be described as mere coincidences. In Hungary, the hearing aid could only be repaired if solder could be found—a commodity which the team searched for in vain in twenty stores. Try demonstrating in sign language your need for solder! Finally, in a tiny back street shop in a remote town halfway across Hungary, the only English-speaking salesman for miles around "happened" to be there when we started our crazy gesticulating. "Don't you mean solder, old chap?" he said. Another tiny miracle! Another answered prayer. Another needy person served.

Each year several short-term mission teams enter Romania, sent by the International Children's Aid Foundation (ICAF). The entire Romanian mission at ICAF began in 1990 after a "chance" encounter I had while changing airplanes at Chicago's O'Hare Airport. The Communist dictator Nicolae Ceaucescu had fallen seven months earlier, and we had been collecting medical supplies and children's clothes for Romania ever since but could not find a worthy, needy recipient. As president of ICAF, I had been warned by authorities not to ship the three and one-half tons of aid unaccompanied. So we arranged passage and even free cargo shipment from an airline. After probably two hundred phone calls around the United States and to Europe, I was three weeks from the deadline that the airline had set as the final shipment date. While waiting at O'Hare for a connecting flight on a business trip, I was studying a Romanian map when a man noticed the map and approached me.

"Are you Romanian?" he asked, slowly.

When I answered I was not, he apologized and explained that a Romanian Christian who had escaped from the communists had joined his church and was now returning to set up a Christian mission there. As he told his story he suddenly glanced at his watch and exclaimed, "Oh, no! That clock on the wall is slow. My flight leaves in three minutes. Gotta go!"

Realizing now that my own flight was leaving in five minutes, I yelled over to him, "Wait! What's the man's name? Where does he live?"

The man quickly shouted the information and dashed off. I was in such a rush to get to my own gate that all I could do was repeat over and over the name and city. When I got to the plane I wrote it on my boarding pass and called the contact when I arrived home.

"Oh, praise the Lord!" he said when I reached him that evening. "Not only can we use everything you have collected, but I will be in Romania the week you arrive. You must stay at my home as our guest." We have gone on to raise tens of thousands of dollars for the mission project, and mission teams have helped build an orphanage, farm, and Christian clinic there. Our world is full of miracles. All we need do is to recognize God's hand in what we frequently pass off as coincidences.

SOME KEY QUESTIONS ABOUT MISSIONS
Short Term or Long Term?

To take a precise view of this chapter's opening sentence, Christ did not specifically challenge us to do *short-term* missions. He has told us to do the work of missions whenever and wherever possible. Yet, the reality is that not many of us have the opportunity to commit to missionary service as a career, and in recent years there has been a marked decline in interest and support in long-term missions. One survey conducted among Southern Baptist congregations ranked foreign missions as the last of the seven priorities listed. The Christian and Missionary Alliance, whose member churches support more than eleven hundred missionaries in sixty nations, has seen the proportion of giving designated to missions drop from 14.7 percent in 1983 to 11.1 percent in 1995. Virtually every international mission agency in North America and Britain has reported an aging donor base that is not being replaced by younger supporters, and a drop in real terms in financial contributions toward career mission worker support. That is the bad news. The good news is that most churches also report a dynamic growth in interest in short-term missions.

The short-term mission is an effective way that we Christians can give our time and talents if we are a nurse, accountant, or bus driver with two to four weeks' annual vacation. Serving during semester breaks or vacation time as volunteers on a mission team is one of life's most rewarding ways of serving God. Short-term mission work gives us the opportunity to grow in our faith and break down the barriers that separate God's people of differing cultures. According to Michael J. Anthony, editor of *The Short-Term Missions Boom,* "By the year 2000, short-termers will make up over 70 percent of all overseas [mission] personnel."[3]

Local, National, Or International?

Chapter 4 will discuss ways of picking the right mission destination for your team. Yet the term *mission trip* often connotes the image of a faraway developing country. Nothing could be further from the truth. There are many mission opportunities around the corner and across the country from your church. Appalachia and rural Mississippi, urban Chicago, New York, Toronto, and Los Angeles are only a few places that spring to mind.

As you read the pointers regarding language training, foreign currency, and so on, these obvious references to international missions are not meant to exclude domestic mission work. The Lord told us to go into "all the world," and that includes our own backyard!

My own church once started a project called "The House that Faith Built"; we committed to rebuild an abandoned house in nearby Camden, New Jersey. Every Saturday morning from May until we turned it over to a homeless family in November, a gang of us showed up and worked. The problem was, we were not much of a team. One person would say, "I have to leave at 11 today." Another would report that he had to miss the next three Saturdays to drive his son to baseball practice. Some would show up one out of every four work days. I am not being critical. Each person gave willingly and generously, and we completed a wonderful project. But we lacked *a focus,* because this was one tiny detail in the maelstrom of work, family, and personal demands that made up our daily lives. If we had taken the volunteers on a bus to a worksite one hundred miles away, we could have concentrated totally on the task at hand, our spiritual reasons for being there, and we all would have benefited from the fellowship of being part of a real team.

BENEFITS TO THE CHURCH

The individuals—both those we are helping and the team members doing the work—benefit from missions, but what about the rest of the congregation? According to Elizabeth Lightbody, missions professor at Moody Bible Institute, "The local church is the key body to encourage and commission short-term missionaries, and to have them report back. That cycle will stimulate people, not just to go, but to give and pray. Short-term missionaries need to know they are their church's ambassadors. The church will get back much more than it gives."[4]

The benefits of a church participating in the missions enterprise is significant. David Hackett, general director of Frontier Mission Fellowship, quotes African Anglican leader Canon Cyril Okorocha: "Any church not involved in missions will soon lose their contact with God and will soon thereafter become targets for other religions' missionaries."

Mission teams energize the church. They instill in the congregation a healthy sense of pride in their church. Not everybody has the time or interest to participate in the work trip, but they should be asked to be partners in the mission by contributing toward the cost, and by praying for the safety and success of the team.

After Trinity Presbyterian Church in Cherry Hill, New Jersey rebuilt an abandoned house on Viola Street in Camden and turned it over to a homeless family, their pastor said, "We built a church on Route 70; we *became* a church on Viola Street." Such was the spirit of caring and sharing that emanated from those Christian laborers.

When my own church launched "The House that Faith Built," we appealed to the congregation for help. Our greatest need was for a construction chairperson, since I did not know which end of a hammer to use. After the worship service at which we made the announcement, a man introduced himself as a professional contractor and volunteered for the job. Dick had been a member of that church for twenty-two years, attending sporadically, never participating in anything other than sitting through the worship service. But the mission project rang his chimes! The next week, a lady approached me, saying that her husband owned a kitchen and bath store and he, too, was interested in helping. He was not even a church member. Because of Dick and Dave, the work project was a resounding success, Dave joined the church, and both men went on to serve the Lord as deacons, members of numerous committees, and today are the heartbeat of our church's mission work.

People get "hooked" on service. In fact, mission teams are good opportunities for people contemplating a life in the ministry. The experience is often a microcosm of a missionary or pastor's life: visiting the sick, dealing with the unexpected, preaching the Gospel, addressing physical needs. "The vast majority of those going into missions today seem to be those who have had some kind of short-term experience," says Moody Graduate School Professor Richard Calenberg. "Short-term mission has become a reality because this generation wants to experience things before they're willing to commit to things."[5]

Even if team members are not headed for the ministry, watching them learn and work together can be a valuable lesson in developing future lay leaders.

A church that is known for sending mission teams will also attract more new members than one that ignores this important challenge. As I write this book, I am still warmed by the experience one month ago when a friend and former coworker showed up at my church one Sunday. "Our family is planning to join the next new members' class," Luray told me after a couple of Sundays. "We love the fact that Faith Church is so involved in hands-on mission."

Luray is just another caring, compassionate human being who feels drawn to the Lord and is filled with joy and inspiration when she sees that other ordinary folks just like her can make a difference in this world in Christ's name. She wants to worship, participate, and join with a church that encourages that type of service.

Your church's members can have a lasting impact. Brooklyn pastor Bill Wilson says each of us can be useful servants, no matter our level of skills:

> I feel more like Edward Kimball [than such famous preachers as Dwight Moody and Billy Graham]. What, you've never heard of

him? Well, if it weren't for Edward Kimball none of those men I mentioned would be in the ministry.

Mr. Kimball was a shoe salesman in Massachusetts. He taught Sunday school every Sunday. God called him to work with the boys in his hometown. One day he got up enough courage to talk to a young boy about Christ. That young boy's name was Dwight. Twenty-one years later Dwight Lyman Moody won to the Lord a young man by the name of F. B. Meyer, who also grew up to be a preacher. An avid enthusiast of personal visitation, Meyer won a young man by the name of J. W. Chapman to Christ. Chapman in turn grew up to be a preacher and brought the message of Christ to a baseball player named Billy Sunday. As an athlete/evangelist, Sunday held a revival in Charlotte, North Carolina, that was so successful that another evangelist by the name of Mordecai Hamm was invited to Charlotte to preach. It was while Hamm was preaching that a teenager named Billy Graham gave his life to Jesus. It all started with a shoe salesman who took the time to develop a relationship with a young boy. Who are the Ed Kimballs today?[6]

Mission workers who make a difference to the unchurched today are not the David Livingstones of Africa, they are the David and Margaret Ramseys of Bulgaria and the Jim Zenkowiches of Romania. The Ramseys had never been on a missions trip, yet they helped to plant churches shortly after Bulgaria left the communist fold. David, an ordained minister, preached with power; Margaret taught little children the stories of God's love. Both brought many into God's kingdom. Meanwhile Jim, a New Jersey mail carrier, unsure how God would use him, gave his testimony early in the first week of his mission trip to Romania. By the second week, he began preaching in churches, and people responded. Jim has returned to Romania three more times, each time putting down his mailbag to pick up his Bible and declare God's love and the need for forgiveness.

David, Margaret, and Jim are not famous; they give their time and money taking the Word to where the opportunities lie. They are not well-known like Billy Graham, commanding a worldwide television audience of millions. Yet, in their obedience to the Great Commission and surrender to the Holy Spirit's leading, they are winning new souls for Christ one at a time. Even with limited skills, God can use you, just as he has the Ramseys and Jim Zenkowich.

OBEDIENCE AND BENEFITS

We started this chapter by stating that the primary reason for sending mission teams from our church is the biblical command to do so. It is so clear and unambiguous:

> Then Jesus came to them and said, "All authority in heaven and on earth has been given to me. Therefore go and make disciples of all nations, baptizing them in the name of the Father and of the Son and of the Holy Spirit, and teaching them to obey everything I have commanded you. And surely I am with you always, to the very end of the age." (Matthew 28:18–20)

Obedience, then, is the key reason for missions service. But our congregations also receive benefits: they will enjoy doing mission work. And those who do not physically participate also can benefit, as they lift up the team with financial and prayer support. Members who help with such "*Fun*-raisers" as a church talent show or craft fair themselves will be drawn into becoming stronger supporters of the church's mission endeavors. Such work will strengthen the faith of the mission team members, encouraging them into service in other areas of church life and enhance the church's reputation in the community as a place that is caring and does fulfilling activities. When the membership feels motivated and fulfilled, there is no telling what the Holy Spirit may lead that congregation to accomplish!

"Why run short-term mission trips?" Because our Lord wants us to; because people need us; because our home church will be enlivened by the activity. "Why should *I* participate?" you ask. Because the mission experience will open your eyes to God's presence in our everyday lives. You will be fulfilling your promise to care for people in need and following directives God set forth in the Bible. Taking part in a mission team will strengthen your faith, touch your heart, deepen your friendships, and change your life.

NOTES

1. Peter C. Wagner, *On the Crest of the Wave* (Glendale, Calif.: Regal, 1983), 5.
2. The stories of Shealey, Harter, and North appear in chapters 9, 2, and 5, respectively, of David C. Forward, *Heroes after Hours* (San Francisco: Jossey-Bass, 1994).
3. Michael J. Anthony, ed., *The Short-Term Missions Boom* (Grand Rapids: Baker, 1994) 237.

4. Elizabeth Lightbody, "More Than a Vacation," *Moody*, November/December 1996, 26.
5. Tamela Baker, "Next in Line," *Moody*, November/December 1996, 21.
6. Bill Wilson and Chris Blake in Anthony, *The Short-Term Missions Boom*, 171.

Chapter Three

※

ARE WE READY
FOR A MISSION TRIP?

*I*n his book *A Mind For Missions,* Paul Borthwick contrasts worldy and world Christians, noting that world Christians are ready to "respond to a world of greater need." Borthwick writes:

> We face a choice to be worldly Christians or world Christians. A worldly Christian is one who accepts the basic message of salvation, but whose lifestyle, priorities, and concerns are molded by the self-centered preoccupation. [The person] looks to the Scripture for personal blessings; prays mostly for immediate, personal needs; and sees the Christian faith as a way to "get God on his side." [1]

A world Christian breaks the mold of a self-centered way of thinking. A world Christian understands that Jesus calls us to deny ourselves (Luke 9:23) so that we might respond to a world of greater need beyond ourselves.

How can you persuade more members of your church to become world Christians? How can you reach those already in that category to increase their support of missions? How do you know if you or your church are ready for a short-term mission trip? The first step is to start looking at the world as God sees it. This chapter contains more questions than answers, but they are issues you must consider before organizing a short-term missions trip for your group.

SHORT-TERM MISSIONS AND YOUR CHURCH

Before you proceed with developing a short-term missions trip, you need to answer the following three questions.

1. Has your church operated short-term missions before? If the answer is yes, it's time for an evaluation, meaning several other questions. What were the results? If the trip(s) went well, what were the main reasons? Was it the team leader, the host, the work they accomplished, the team itself? If the experience was not so good, evaluate why. Did you have a debriefing session after the last trip? What were the participants' comments and suggestions?
2. If your church has not previously run a short-term mission trip, why are you considering it now?
3. Are there other problems in the church presently that might affect the mission trip's success?

COMMON OBJECTIONS TO SHORT-TERM MISSION

Do not expect unanimous support and accolades for your short-term mission proposals. Some members of your church (like most churches) probably will question and hesitate. Here are some of the most common objections to short-term missions, along with suitable responses you can offer:

1. "You are interfering with the work of the professionals." *Response:* The traditional paradigm in the mission field has changed. Where the acceptable form of spreading the Gospel was once to send out ordained career missionaries for decades at a time, today the cost and the sensitivities in the host countries make that a less desirable approach. Today, a partnership between career missionaries, the host community church, and short-termers offers an optimal combination of support, energy, and self-empowerment. In fact, many career missionaries report increased support as a result of

their teamwork with short termers.

2. "It is more cost-effective to just send our money to the denomination/field." *Response:* We are not quantifying missions on cost alone. The main purpose is to develop servant-disciples within our group. Another is to influence them to consider mission work as a career. Yet another benefit of experiencing missions "live" is the increase in future support for missions from participants.

3. "It costs too much." *Response:* People will spend thousands of dollars on tickets to sporting events, dinners at fancy restaurants, and other luxuries over the course of a year. You may ask parents and church leaders the following honest questions: "How much have we spent on items from CD recordings to gourmet coffee in the last year, compared with what we spent on supporting the Lord's work overseas? How much do we willingly spend on computer software to educate ourselves and our children? A mission trip is perhaps the one learning experience that can have a lifelong effect on those who participate—adults and teens alike.

4. "Why travel that far when there are needs closer to home?" *Response:* Jesus' command was to take His Word into all the world. Tell those who object that the mission team will be entering a community in which there is a specific, identified opportunity to witness for Him and to serve people in need. Then add, "We are going at the invitation of local mission experts who feel we can make a real difference to their community, and believe the focused, dedicated team, working together in that community, can have an impact. If you have identified similar needs close to home, I encourage you to do something tangible to address them."

MEETING WITH CHURCH
COMMITTEES AND FORMING THE TEAM
Meeting with the Committee

You have addressed the questions above and decide to proceed. The next step varies from church to church, depending on the organizational structure. Sometimes the senior pastor has the authority to initiate the project. In others, it might require approval by the bishop, mission committee, board of elders, or church council.

Before approaching those committees, remember that the members may not have the benefit of the fire you feel burning inside you for the trip. Where you see opportunities to serve people in need, committee members may anticipate expenses the church cannot afford, sickness among the team, and liability for the church. You should put yourself in their position and contemplate the questions you would have if you were safeguarding the interests of the church and the team members. Be prepared to answer the following questions:

1. Exactly how much will it cost?
2. How are you going to raise that money?
3. How many people will you take?
4. What if you drop below that number? Is there a minimum or maximum group size?
5. Will the agency (or you, if going independently of an agency) allow youth participants? What ages?
6. What are the sleeping arrangements?
7. Who will be responsible for chaperoning the teens?
8. Will nonchurch members be permitted?
9. What if a participant is injured or seriously ill during the trip?
10. What other resources will you need? How will they be paid for?

Set the tone for this discussion by referring to the biblical basis for missions, as covered in chapter 1. Remember, too, that a primary goal is the spiritual development of the members of your team. Longtime missions activist Jack Larson writes,

> Keep in mind that the goal of your short-term mission experience is not the project itself. The project that you select to invest in is actually a means to accomplishing your goal. The goal of a short-

term missions activity is for the church leader to disciple his or her volunteers. A project may last for a few brief weeks, but the relationship that you build with your volunteers will last for years to come.[2]

Forming the Core of Your Team

As you consider forming the team, think the trip through in great detail. For this example, let's say you are planning a trip to Mexico to help build a chapel at an orphanage. You also want to hold vacation Bible schools in five different villages, preach each evening in different settings, and take some health-care professionals on the team to provide free consultations to impoverished people in the host community.

For this mission, you might decide you want *at least* nine people in your core group: two to plan the Vacation Bible School (VBS), a construction coordinator, someone to take charge of the health care, and probably two more folks from the congregation who could be responsible for generating donations of building and medical supplies from local sources in your home community. You might want a musically talented person to plan, translate, and teach the team the songs they will sing in Spanish during your worship times during the trip. Another person with experience in fund-raising would be an invaluable addition. Finally, you might look for a gregarious, well-respected member who would be responsible for recruiting the mission team from the congregation. (If the pastor will join the team, he is a natural choice. See the section below "Promotion by the Core Team Members" on the pastor's role.)

Once you have secured approval from your church leaders to run the trip, you need to assemble your core group of participants. You cannot possibly be responsible for all aspects of a mission trip yourself. No matter how many people have told you that you do a wonderful job, you are not invincible. You may have participated in previous mission teams, traveled extensively, and hold a position of power in your profession: yet when your team gets to the construction site, you become the lowly gofer! You have to delegate the tasks to people who are better qualified to complete them. "When it's time for VBS," as my associate pastor says, "I don't do glitter."

While it is important to delegate from a human resource standpoint, it is also crucial that you recognize and utilize the differing gifts with which the team members have been blessed. Don't look just at their vocational skills: the carpenter will probably be a good builder and the pastor a suitable preacher. But when you poll the team, you will probably discover the nurse who wants to do construction, the mail carrier who feels the call to preach, and the retired housewife who wants to lead adult Bible study for senior citizens.

From this simple mission project, you can see how, without nine reliable, motivated people in your core group, your mission trip is destined to fail in some key areas—unless you devote umpteen additional hours of your own time. Look again at the title of this chapter. If you filled most of the key-person vacancies with your own name, you are probably not ready to operate a mission team.

However, although you now have your nine-person core group, *you* are the team leader. Having just made the point of delegating many tasks to team members, you cannot allow true democracy to rule every decision. With the nine core members and many other team members, you may have twenty volunteers or more. Your twenty-person group will have twenty differing reasons for going on this mission, twenty separate recommendations on when and where it should go, and perhaps twenty varying ideas on what the team should do when they get there. If you encourage the notion that every decision will be made democratically, you are not running the trip—the trip is running you! There is no need to enlist opinions on such things as whether to fly Swissair or Lufthansa. In fact, even putting the destination to a vote might cause the minority to later use that as a reason to gripe about how "this wouldn't have happened if we had gone to X instead of Y."

Promotion by the Core Team Members

Your church pastor may promote the mission from the pulpit long and loud. But he also is very busy. As you assemble the team you might look for a different person, perhaps someone who is gregarious and well-respected, who can lead the recruiting of the remaining mission team members from the congregation.

Promotion for the short-term mission trip can take many forms. A "Missions Sunday" with encouragement from the pulpit and bulletin inserts weeks before, is a good way to attract attention to the trip. Have one or two team members at an information table after the service to answer questions and distribute basic information. (The more detailed information comes at the preliminary "kick-off meeting"; see chapter 6). Coordinate the Missions Sunday with an article in your church newsletter and perhaps even a simultaneous approach to members of a nearby church with whom your own church enjoys a relationship.

Clearly, the ideal is for the senior pastor to enthusiastically support your short-term mission—preferably as a participant. Most members are often attracted to join the team when they see their pastor is going along. Yet sometimes that is not possible. Maybe scheduling conflicts prevent him from going. Some pastors just do not feel called to that kind of work, yet they will strongly endorse the idea of a team from their church. Others will be less enthusiastic. "It's like these are the scales of justice," one minister gestured, "and here is evangelism (holding his right hand up to his head), and here is missions (holding his left hand down around his waist). Even in that case, where the pastor could not be counted on to initiate or overtly support his church's mission activities, he was happy to let the mission-oriented members of his congregation conduct a fairly active missions program.

The key here is to realize that the mandate for missions comes from God, not man. You may be blessed with a pastor who is delighted that some members want to promote missions to the congregation and will promote the idea in every way. But if that is not the case, remember your opportunity for directing the effort, as expressed in the little ten-word phrase of two letters each: "If it is to be, it is up to me."

THE MOTIVES OF TEAM MEMBERS

Each team member should ask himself: *What is my motivation for even contemplating this trip? Am I going primarily for my own benefit, or for that of others? Has an overzealous friend made me feel compelled to go? Does the excitement of a trip to a distant foreign land appeal to me?* Sometimes a person's conscience nags him into thinking, *I'd better go, because I owe it to God.* Although such thoughts often enter our minds, none of them is a good reason to participate in a mission trip!

If you are planning to join a short-term missions team, be committed to the project. Don't go just because a friend asks you to join him or her. Thinking your participation will please someone else (or God) is the worst reason to join a mission team. Work trips are no vacation; deciding without a full commitment on your part can result in some decidedly unpleasant moments when the going gets tough and you are far from home. Nor should you join a mission team just because it offers a trip to a far-away destination.

Having given those warnings, I recognize that God can move people's hearts during a mission. You may have heard from many who say they never felt so refreshed than after their return from a mission work trip where they have slogged away in the hot sun for ten days. They return to work glowing with personal gratification and appreciation for the opportunity of spending so much focused time helping others and in close communication with the Lord and His other faithful servants. Their perspective is changed; they have a new zeal for service. As one participant told me, "I've been on several cruises where you spend every day lounging by the pool, gorging yourself on endless sumptuous meals, and return to work feeling exhausted, guilty, and bloated! When I came back from a mission work trip, I was happy, satisfied, relaxed—and it made all the silly frustrations we encounter in the office seem unimportant."

We all know the Lord loves a cheerful giver. We also know that God does not need anything from us; we cannot earn our way into His kingdom by spending lots of money and taking mission trips. As to your attitude, this is the time to be brutally honest with yourself. Do you really feel the Holy Spirit is working in your heart, urging you to go? Although the team leader needs to feel the compelling call that it is the Lord's wish for him or her to lead the group, do not expect every team member to appear as excited. It is only natural for some to appear a little apprehensive about the experience. Others do not discover the calling until they are actually on the trip, witnessing the needs and the people in the host community. The team leader's job is to ascertain whether applicants for the team either have the ability now, or might later discover their calling, to share their talents and faith with others who are not as blessed.

If you are considering joining the mission trip, read Mark 1:14–18. (If you are the leader, ask prospective team members to read this Scripture passage.) The passage describes the time Jesus came upon the brothers Simon and Andrew as they were fishing in the Sea of Galilee. "Come, follow me," He said. Such a simple command. And such faith of the two men to leave everything they owned and follow Him. It serves to remind us to follow what we believe is the call of Jesus in times of doubt about which way we should go.

Martin Luther once said, "I don't know which road to take, but how well I know who my guide will be." Not long after earning my pilot's license, I was flying with another pilot one snowy, winter day to Erie, Pennsylvania. As we were being blown all over the Pennsylvania mountains, I asked my copilot to plot a more direct course. After twenty minutes of leaving it up to him, I realized something was wrong. Finally I asked to see the map myself. And then I discovered our error: my copilot was using the wrong map! It was an early lesson in relying more on the guide than on a map. The same holds true in this discussion. Like Luther, we know well our Guide. Place your questions at the feet of the Guide and ask Him to lead your heart to the decision that is right for you.

You cannot follow any magic formula to prove whether you should go on the missions trip. Yet careful, prayerful soul-searching will almost certainly provide the answer. Several months after she had signed up for a mission team, Carol called the team leader and asked if she could visit him that evening. An officer in her church and a very experienced nurse, Carol had participated in previous travel and missions work in developing countries. In short, she looked like the ideal candidate to serve the host community. When she poured out her heart that evening, she told how she thought she should cancel because her father had "gone ballistic" over her intention to travel to Bulgaria. It was during the worst part of the civil war in Bosnia, and his concern was that the conflict could roll into the adjacent mission destination.

The team leader thought that was a ridiculous fear, one without foundation, but he had to refrain from "selling her" on staying on the team. Wisely, he did. As mission team leaders, our mandate does not include urging people to override their father's wishes—even when members are fifty years old! Carol and the team leader discussed the facts of the geography and politics of the region, they talked about her role, and they studied at length the biblical basis for missions.

Carol agreed to pray on her dilemma and went home. A day or so later she called to say she felt the Lord had answered her, and that He was telling her it was His will to stay on the team. Carol went to Bulgaria and made some substantial contributions to the team, the poor and suffering in the host community, and to her own walk of faith with the Lord.

I can think of half a dozen teenagers who joined our mission teams and whom we insisted think carefully through the steps described above. They attended all pre-trip training sessions and everyone involved believed they were ready for the experience. Some of my fondest memories are of those young people thousands of miles from home, in a culture completely alien to them, rising to the challenges God sent for them: Nathan leading the songs at VBS; Julie jumping right into a conflict that erupted between others and being a peacemaker; Jamie using her artistic talent to paint Winnie the Pooh characters on the orphanage walls; Jennifer and Anne—scared to death—running wonderfully successful VBSs in the villages.

The tougher times occur when that inner feeling tells you that you (or another team member) are not ready for the trip. One team member took his eleven-year-old grandson along, and because he lived far away, the child never attended a single training meeting. Who knows what decisions the boy made, but I suspect "a neat trip" was the primary reason he went. Honestly, the child was no problem on the team, but he made no contribution. He never interacted with local children. He stood around during the vacation Bible schools—actually, he spent most of the trip standing around watching. He was a great kid, I am sure. But when I think of the Lord's challenge for us to be good stewards of our resources, I wince at the fact someone spent $1,300 for this child's trip. The same amount could have been used to pay a doctor's salary at our clinic for a year. I should have encouraged the parents and the child to discuss and prayerfully consider the same question this chapter asks: "Are you ready for this mission trip?" The only honest answer could have been, "Not yet."

Ask yourself that question. If the answer is yes, get ready for an exciting adventure in the service of Jesus.

NOTES

1. Paul Borthwick, *A Mind For Missions* (Colorado Springs: NavPress, 1987), 13.
2. Jack Larson in Michael J. Anthony, ed., *The Short-Term Missions Boom* (Grand Rapids: Baker, 1994), 114–15.

Chapter Four
※
GETTING STARTED

$\mathcal{F}$rom the exercises in previous chapters, you have decided to proceed with a mission trip. You also might have a fairly good idea about what your team will do when it arrives at the host community. Let us develop that thought further.

The kinds of activities occurring on mission trips can be varied. In addition to evangelism and assisting missionaries with church planting, activities can include:

- Teaching the Bible and preaching.
- Giving medical care, both directly for patients or teaching the local practitioners skills and techniques in modern medicine.
- Constructing new buildings, renovating dilapidated structures.
- Teaching Vacation Bible School, English as a second language, nutrition, business, or agriculture skills.
- Providing child care in orphanages or with street kids.
- Helping locals to identify and market their strengths and abilities. This provides the self-sufficiency and even sustenance reflected in the saying, "Give a man a fish and you feed him for a day; teach him how to fish and you feed him for a lifetime."
- Helping local aid-providers get organized: personnel, bookkeeping, finances.

Both the abilities and expectations of your team members will influence the activities you can engage in. Will your group have many people with one specific skill, such as doctors or builders? If so, is it your intention to focus on just one or two activities, such as "Provide dentistry to every child we can reach," or "Build this specific structure"? Be sure to ask team members what their expectations are of the upcoming mission. Why do they want to go? What do they have to contribute to the work once in the host community? Assume nothing. Just because Chris is a builder should not lead you to believe that he wants to work in that field during the trip; Jill is one registered nurse with vast experience but who likes to go on mission trips so she can work in construction. Determining their desires and interests early will help you know what projects are realistic—and will help you from making false assumptions and having frustrated members of the team.

WHERE SHOULD YOUR TEAM GO?

Sometimes your decisions are governed more by geographic preferences: "Our associate pastor is from Guatemala, so we want to send a team there." When you plan the mission, you might want to have several goals rather than one or two specialized tasks.

An old saw says, "The first rule of marketing is: find a need, then fill it." The problem for mission team planners is that there is a big world out there, and it is filled with needs. So where do you start? In his insightful book, *A Mind for Missions,* Paul Borthwick passes on the advice he learned from his seminary missions professor: "The Bible tells us what God wants to do in the world; the newspaper tells us where He needs to do it and where we need to be involved through our prayers. From that day on," Borthwick notes "I have taken a greater interest in local and world news."[1] In addition to reading about current events, you can learn about world needs through other readings. William Carey, the father of modern missions, got his inspiration and drive for foreign missions from reading secular literature: *Captain Cook's Voyages.*

If you do not already have a connection with one region or country, why not ask your core group for suggestions. A missions team from a Baptist church in Dallas decided to focus on Russia after they learned that their pastor was about to adopt two babies from Russia. A Presbyterian church from Charlotte chose Colombia after hearing news reports of a recent earthquake that had shattered thousands of lives and completely destroyed many villages. Another church team proposed Rwanda and Bosnia, seeing themselves as missionaries promoting the continuation of peace to those war-torn nations; others had family ties in Mexico and the Philippines. And two other church groups chose Moldavia and Ukraine, respectively, wanting to strengthen the new democracies and fledgling Christian communities in those countries.

Team leaders should be careful not to imply that the team will adopt any one person's suggestion. Instead, stress that their nomination will be considered seriously and report back after you have researched the possibilities. In the preceding examples, they ruled out the Philippines because the airfare from the U.S. East Coast was too high; they skipped Rwanda after the State Department and other sources reported the military situation was still extremely dangerous—Western aid workers and missionaries were still being mistreated and even killed there.

By this point, you have decided where to go: let us say that choice is to Brazil. You have also sharpened the focus of your team to working with children. You have a doctor and two nurses who are interested in joining the group to provide health care. The team will number about twenty people, with no concentration of any one skill among the remaining members. You have no contacts in Brazil.

RESEARCH ON YOUR CHOSEN DESTINATION

Start a file in which you can store information you collect on your mission destination. Excellent sources of background information on international destinations are:

- The Internet.
- Libraries.
- U.S. government country profiles. The U.S. Departments of State and Commerce both make their extensive reports on each country available. You can access this information from large county libraries and those at major universities.

- The Embassy of the country itself. More than one hundred countries have their embassies in our nation's capital. You can get their address and phone number by calling directory assistance in Washington, D. C. (202-555-1212), and asking for the particular embassy's address and telephone number. (Many larger libraries also have telephone books of large U.S. cities, including Washington.) Keep in mind an embassy's literature will be written from their own political perspective.
- Newspapers and magazines.
- Encyclopedias.
- "Culturgrams," brief synopses of the language, culture, and statistics of 153 countries, published by the Kennedy Center for International Studies at Brigham Young University.[2]

You should attempt to contact a career missionary who is (or was recently) based in your intended destination. The world missions departments at denominational headquarters can probably refer you to specific people, as will the mission yearbook or directory which many denominations publish annually.

A source of good information on the traditions and cultures of developing nations is often the students from those countries who are studying in the United States. If you are close to a large, internationally known university, call them and ask how you can get in touch with students from a specific country, and they are usually pleased to make the connection for you. An international student studying in America is also an excellent person to invite to your team meeting just before you leave for the group to engage in "live" language practice. Invite a native of Brazil to your final meeting, and you will have good practice in speaking Portuguese. Leave time for the student to answer your group's questions (and perhaps to discuss some of his or her favorite customs).

WHEN SHOULD YOU GO?

You have learned what to do and where you will go. You have valuable background information on the country. Now there is the question of timing: When should you run the trip? Your core group feedback has told you that they prefer summertime. You consider June, July, and August for the missions trip to Brazil. Early June is likely to clash with families who take vacations right after the school year ends. The youth pastor has advised you of four high school seniors and college freshmen who want to join the team, but they will be attending colleges that start their semesters in the third week of August. We are down to a mid-June to early August "window." You visit the library and when looking up "Brazil," you see national holidays on June 17 and 26. Forget June.

It is time to call the cultural attaché at the Brazilian Embassy or consulate. Tell the official what you are doing and seek advice. During the conversation, the attaché mentions, "*Everybody* in Brazil goes on vacation in August." While it is true that the street kids and orphans your team will be ministering to do not take vacations, other people whom you might want to contact during the trip probably will be away then.

So you have July. When you talk with your travel provider, ask if you can save money by flying on off-peak days (and ask what those days are, in their case). One team saved $180 per person by flying out on a Thursday instead of Friday—that was a $4,320 saving for the twenty-four-person group. With your restricted (but less expensive) departure day, you now have a manageable range of dates: say, out on July 8, 15, or 22 and home on July 16, 23, or 30. Many mission experts try to plan their trips to arrive at the host community on Saturday evening. That way, their first bonds will be formed while worshiping with their hosts on Sunday. It is generally a slow day, with little or no heavy work done, so the team can compensate for their travel fatigue. But more importantly, it illustrates that the physical work is secondary, coming as an outcome of their worshiping and fellowshiping together with their Christian partners.

FINDING THE RIGHT HOST

You have your country, your team's work focus, and your dates. Now how do you find the right mission to host your team? The "Guide to Selected Short-Term Mission Opportunities" (Appendix G) lists more than two dozen agencies that host short-term mission teams. They are listed alphabetically, and by geographic region and specialty of skills needed. Look at the cross-reference chart on page 230–31. If you have a group of dentists wanting to provide their expertise on a medical mission, you can hone right in on the organizations able to host such teams. One caveat: this information was accurate at the book's writing. However, telephone numbers, mission objectives, and many other facts might have changed by the time you call. Pick two or three organizations that interest you, and contact them. Tell them about your group, what the team wants to do, along with the dates and locations you have identified. If they are active in those areas, ask them to send you printed material on their organization, what they can offer your group, and how other teams like yours have served in their communities previously. Try to learn some history of how they have taught (and received) the Gospel in the country you plan to visit.

If you use a missions consultant or specialist, all of the above research should be done for you. The specialist will ascertain from one of your first conversations what type of team you anticipate and will present you with one or more reliable host sites that meet your criteria.

By this time, you should have reached a consensus with the mission host on:

- The size limits for your team
- The dates
- Costs
- What type of work the team will undertake during their stay
- Who is responsible for providing such necessities as accommodations, meals, and translators

A final thought: Consider bringing a national alongside each member during the trip. Let's assume your primary goal is to build a structure, or dig an irrigation system while at your mission site in Haiti. Instead of the team doing all the work, while there is 40 percent local unemployment, why not build in a small additional amount to everybody's trip cost and hire a buddy to work alongside each team member? In many developing countries, unskilled workers earn $15 to $20 per week—a tiny amount to furnish someone the self-esteem of a paycheck.

Money will be on the minds of your own team members, of course, as they consider the cost of the upcoming trip. We will learn "all about money" and anticipating accurately the costs of the mission in chapter 5.

NOTES

1. Paul Borthwick, *A Mind for Missions* (Colorado Springs: NavPress, 1987), 44.
2. Write the David M. Kennedy Center for International Studies, Publication Services, Brigham Young University, 280 HRCB, Provo, UT 84602; telephone: 801-378-6528. Culturgrams are available individually or in sufficient quantity for the entire team. There is a charge.

Chapter Five

ALL ABOUT MONEY

*T*here are many costs to a missions trip—not just financial ones. Team leaders and participants should realize the personal costs. Time and schedules are disrupted and rearranged. Members must expend energy in learning a language and coping with cultural differences. During the mission, the sheer work of ministry, often in uncomfortable conditions, is a major cost.

Yet these contributions of your time and talents are matched by the need for you to share your treasures. It is these financial costs, which require much planning, that this chapter addresses.

How do you establish the price that participants should pay for their mission trip? Besides the obvious answer of adding up the individual component costs—airfare, room and board, and so forth—here are some questions to consider:

- Are taxes included in your airfare quote? How about airport exit taxes (including security charges)? They can add as much as $50 per person on international flights.
- What about taxes (often called "valued added taxes," or VAT) in your host country? Many countries have this "national sales tax" which can be enormous: in some Canadian provinces it totals 17 percent, Britain's is 17.5 percent, in Hungary it is 25 percent!
- Do you need to add the cost of a bus from your church to the airport and return?

- Are all meals and accommodations included, or do you need to factor in en route rooms or meals, for example?
- Do you want to make a financial gift to the hosting mission? Does that need to be prorated among the group?
- Have you included travel insurance? The safest way to ensure total enrollment is to include the premium in the package price—but that could add $100 to each person's bill. You can save money with group rates, too.
- Are any of the international components quoted in foreign currency? If so, see the section below on "currency risk."
- Should anyone's airfare be free, such as a translator's ? If so, be sure to divide the individual's cost by the remaining team members and add that amount as a cost item.
- Should you buy small gifts for your hosts and people you might meet during the trip?
- Do you need to factor in a cost for buying supplies, such as for the VBS or construction project?
- Have you been conservative in prorating costs? For example, if the quotation for a bus is $2,000 and you figure your team will be twenty persons, you know it will cost $100 per person. However, if everybody has paid in full and you go out with only twelve people, you cannot very well go back and ask them for an additional $67 each. Always divide such costs into the "worst case" number you can imagine.

After calculating the cost of the trip, take a few moments in a quiet place and "think" your way through the entire expedition. Imagine the months before departure and "see" anything the group might need: language phrase books, for example. (Should we buy them in bulk and give one to everybody?) Then think through the day of departure: getting to the airport (Do we need a bus?), checking in (Do we need to tip sky caps or will everyone carry their own bags?), the flight (no extra costs there), arrival at the destination airport, going through customs (Visas! Do we need visas?), and lots of luggage coming off the carousel (Is it easier to load them all onto one big cart and pay a porter to wheel them to the bus?). Do the same with day two—we are teaching a

VBS in the morning (we will need crayons, Bible storybooks in Portuguese, and balloons), etc.—and for each subsequent day.

As you think your way through every day of the trip, it is easy to anticipate little expenses here and there that, when multiplied by twenty people and compounded, can really add up. Even if you elect not to include these items, you will be a better group leader by informing your team members ahead of the extra expenses they may incur.

CURRENCY RISK

When planning an overseas mission, you must deal with the additional complication of a foreign currency. Every minute of every day, the world's currencies are fluctuating in value. Some developing nations' currencies tend to continuously devalue against the U.S. dollar, so there is not much currency risk to Americans. In August 1994, Romania's currency, the *lei*, were exchanged at the rate of 300 *lei* for every U.S. dollar. Two years later, in August 1996, each dollar bought 3,400 *lei*. By August 1997 the exchange rate had doubled again to 8,000 *lei* to the dollar. Such devaluation and rampant inflation put the greatest strain on the country's neediest people—the poor and the elderly. For Americans abroad, though, this means their money will at least retain (and sometimes increase) its value where inflation exists. That also has been the situation in Mexico and several South American countries.

In contrast, consider a mission trip to Hungary. The country also has suffered through inflation. But businesses such as hotels, restaurants, and bus companies frequently quote their foreign clients not in Hungarian *forints*, but in deutsche marks. Now we have a problem, because in recent years the U.S. dollar has lost value against the mark. Let us review a hypothetical example.

The travel agent quotes you the following for your twenty-person, seven-night mission trip to Debrecen, Hungary next summer:

10 rooms @ deutsche marks (DM) 90 per night	= DM 6,300
Seven days' meals @ DM30 per day (estimated)	= DM 4,200
Buses from Budapest airport to Debrecen & back	= DM 880
Total cost:	= DM 11,380

You check today's newspaper and see the deutsche mark is listed at 1.65 to the dollar. How do you price the trip? Be careful: 11,380 divided by 1.65 equals $6,897, but the currency exchange rates you see in the newspaper are those the huge global banks and currency traders use when transferring tens of millions of dollars every day. You and I will never get that rate on an individual exchange. To get a more realistic rate, call a bank or exchange bureau and ask for the current average retail rate—including their service charges.

Now assume you find the retail exchange rate is 1.60 DM to the dollar. Your calculation yields costs for those land arrangements of $7,113. Our price has already gone up $216 and we have not yet left home!

Months pass. When the team is finally ready to leave, you enter the bank the day before the trip and ask for a foreign currency draft for 11,380 German marks. "Certainly," your friendly banker says. "That will be $7,438, please." You protest and show her your calculation. She explains that the dollar has fallen in value, compared with the mark, and is now trading at 1.53. You have to come up with *another* $325. The Hungarians have not raised their prices, they simply quoted you in a hard currency that increased in value. Be very careful with rates quoted in foreign currency, especially the D-mark, Austrian *schilling,* Japanese *yen,* French or Swiss *franc,* and British pound.

Some planners would simply ask everybody to cough up the additional money. However, even on occasions when you have warned your group there might be a fuel surcharge or similar extra levy, they will not like it when you come to collect.

What can you do to safeguard your precious resources against these nasty surprises? Build in a safety factor at the time you originally price the trip: use either a lower exchange rate or build in a $20 to $30 amount for miscellaneous expenses. If the anticipated cost escalations never happen, you have a small fund for tips, ice cream for the children, goodies for the VBS, etc.

A final tip for calculating the cost of another currency. One World Wide Web site offers a valuable free service by providing an instant conversion among 164 currencies. To access it, use their Internet address: http://www.oanda.com/cgi-bin/ncc.

THE TIME FOR PAYMENT

When should the team leader request payment? I suggest you always ask participants to make a deposit—even if it is only $100—early on. Although you can make it refundable if they need to cancel before you send money to service providers, experience has shown that this token payment separates serious team members from those who are "just looking." Few things are more disheartening and frustrating than having seven of your sixteen team members drop out sixty days before you leave, when you ask them for money. It is probably too late to find replacements for them so close to departure and the entire trip could be jeopardized.

As each service provider quotes his cost, ask him when he requires payment. The accumulated answers will help you decide whether, when, and how much the team members should pay in installments. When you do have staged payments to make to vendors before you leave, always give team members a due date two weeks before the day you have to pay your service provider. Also, if you will need to wire-transfer funds to overseas vendors, be sure to factor in bank fees, which can easily be $50 per transfer.

If your team will be involved in a project that will require purchasing supplies, such as construction items, planting crops, or teaching materials, bear in mind the local host may not have the money to buy those supplies before you arrive. You should discuss this with your host and see if you should remit enough for them to buy the materials in advance so your team can get to work upon arrival. One team leader discovered their local host did not have sufficient money to purchase bricks for the very construction project the team planned to build. By sending over sufficient funds in advance, he arranged for the bricks to be delivered just before the work team arrived, avoiding a frustrating three-day wait.

HOW SHOULD THE MISSION TRIP BE PAID FOR?

There are several ways to pay for a mission trip. Four common approaches are:

1. Each individual pays for himself or herself.
2. The church mission budget pays for the entire team.
3. Scholarships are awarded based on need.

4. Some combination of the first three.

Let's look at the benefits and disadvantages of the first three approaches. As you look at the pros and cons, consider the needs and specific situation in your church.

Individual Responsibility For Payment

Pro. This is easy to administer—just keep a log of each team member's payment. It also avoids criticism and unsolicited words of wisdom from the congregation, because no church money is being used.

Con. Particularly on more expensive trips, it separates the haves from the have-nots. This policy could exclude a person who could make a meaningful impact on the very people your mission is going to help from the team because they cannot afford the trip. (That's why a popular option of this is to raise financial support from friends, family, and church members. See "Raising Funds.")

The Church Pays for the Entire Team

Pro. No one will be denied from participating based on his or her personal financial ability. Church and team leaders may feel they can exert more control over the team's activities.

Con: Church budgets are often set ahead of the typical decision to operate a mission trip, so there may not be enough in the current budget. Full disclosure to the congregation could lead to negative comments about how "their" tithes and offerings are being spent. Everybody has their own ideas about whether and where the trip should take place. Because of the minimal personal cost, more applicants may want to join the team than there are spaces available. The selection process is time consuming and may lead to dissent when some church members are selected over others.

Scholarships to Those in Need

Pro. This method allows those who are willing and able to pay for themselves to do so, while providing the financial assistance to permit other worthy participants with the means to join the team. While the group is forming, you would announce the trip price, then ask anybody who might require financial assistance to apply for it.

Their application could be as informal as a telephone call, or as formal as a scholarship application. Before that announcement, you need to decide how you will handle such requests. Will the team leader, church treasurer, or pastor alone decide whom to approve, and for what amount, or will a subcommittee rule on these scholarship applications? Direct grants from the church, individual sponsors, or fund-raising programs can fulfill those scholarships.

Con. Depending on the number of people and the declared amount of need, the funds may be limited. And occasionally, one member with a sincere desire to go and limited resources may need almost all his costs covered; this could limit the remainder of the fund. (Two solutions are having them raise some financial support and/or increasing the scholarship fund through innovative fund-raising programs. (See the subsequent sections "Raising Funds" and "Fund-raising Ideas.")

RAISING FUNDS

When the entire church becomes involved in mission funding, the burdens are shared, but so are the rewards. When the team leaves, they will benefit from a multiplicity of prayer partners; when they return, the congregation listens with interest and pride to their report.

Some might argue that between the annual stewardship campaign and many other special offerings and appeals throughout the year, church members may react adversely to a request for funds for a mission trip. Yet experience has shown that congregations respond well to mission campaigns that are explained well. Of course, some people will complain about anything. Remember to specifically point out that the mission trip is the beneficiary of the fund-raiser.

It is not enough to stand up on Sunday and quote a few statistics, throw in a Bible verse or two, and wait for the money to pour in. Like a memorable sermon—like the parables Jesus told—you need to tell a story that touches human emotions of the listener and challenges them to become part of the solution.

Writing Letters

Another popular method of raising money is for team members to write to friends, family, even other church members, asking for support. A church in Annapolis, Maryland, even mandates that *all* team members raise their mission trip costs this way; they are not allowed to simply write a check, even if they are financially capable of doing so. Their pastor explains that it is an important lesson in humility, and puts every team member on the same footing. Maybe so. Yet some people would refuse to participate in a team if they had to do that. Nonetheless, the Annapolis church has an active missions program with no problems enlisting team members. If you do select this method, be sure to keep your letter to one page, make it personal, not a form letter, and discuss in advance with the team how to avoid sending more than one request to the same person. Team members can handle this last point either by agreeing to share between them a gift from shared friends, or to "trade off": "You send a letter to Sally, then, and I will send one to Joe."

Direct mail fund-raising experts consider the medium to have two primary purposes: You can reach many potential donors whom you cannot contact personally, and it is a targeted, relatively inexpensive method of getting your message out to a large audience. Here are four valuable tips for any mailing team members send asking for financial support.

- Once opened, a personal letter has ten seconds to capture the reader's attention. Mass-produced typed letters only have five seconds. The P. S. always stands out and is often read first. It should contain the deadline, the action you are seeking, and any specific amount you are requesting.
- Avoid long words and sentences. Shoot for words averaging five letters and short, conversational sentences and paragraphs free of technical or jargon words.
- Eighty percent of all donations (in large bulk mailing campaigns) come from 5 percent of the donors.
- Mention dollar amounts several times in the letter.

One Christian organization that helps the needy, Habitat for Humanity, requires members of its short-term work teams in its Global Village partnership to contribute $350 per person toward the construction costs of their chosen project. While many people vow they would never write letters asking for financial support for their trip expenses, few are opposed to the suggestion that they request contributions toward the project cost. One team member's letter to friends asking for support for the construction costs of an orphanage in Transylvania brought more than $6,000 in response.

Visualizing the Need

People like to give to causes they can visualize. Stewardship folks can stand up and quote verse after verse of Scripture that explain the importance of giving to the church—with miserable results. They see all those eyes looking up and are tempted to ask, "Are you listening? This isn't me talking. These are the words of our Lord Himself!" When the pledge cards come in, many show little or no increase from the amount pledged last year, and the year before that.

Yet tell the congregation about Timothy, the crippled boy from Malawi on whom your missionary doctors performed surgery; about the women in the Peruvian village who had used "seed" money from your church to start a crafts cooperative, which now earns them profits from which they can feed their whole families—and the pledges and checks come flowing in with unparalleled generosity. So tell the story of your mission team: why you are going, what your dreams are, and visualize the need by describing the people.

In your letter or presentation tell how they can help you reach those goals. You do not need more than a couple of minutes to make your point.

There is an often-told story of notorious bank robber Willy Sutton, who, when the police finally captured him was asked why he had robbed so many banks. "Because that's where the money is," he replied. Please do not fund your mission trips by robbing banks! The illustration is made to point out that your best chance of getting mission funds is to ask for them in the right places. Your mailing list of friends, family, and church members is the right place. And the results, after proper preparation and prayer, will show God's involvement in your ministry.

One Sunday afternoon a church member called a mission team leader at home on a men's fellowship matter. During their conversation, the leader happened to mention the upcoming mission trip and how two people would probably have to drop out because their fund-raising results had been disappointing. "How much do you need?" asked the caller. The team leader told him the trip cost $1,400 per person. Twenty minutes later the young man called back: "I just spoke with a family member," he reported. "She will give me a check for $2,800 tomorrow and I'll drop it off at the church." A pastor and one of the church's most talented teens were thus able to make significant contributions to that mission team all because of a casual mention of the human side of the mission story to a person who took it to the donor—someone who was not even a member of the church.

FUND-RAISING IDEAS

There are many ways a church can raise funds for its mission team. All of them can be fun, and during their promotion, they can make church members and attenders aware of the group's goals and needs. For example, the youth of Miami Shores Presbyterian Church of Florida sells shares in their mission trips, mimicking the way investment partners raise money. "Shareholders" receive a postcard from the team during the trip, reports youth director Ruben Velasco. When the team returns, members mail invitations to a special dinner and slide presentation. They present each shareholder a small gift from the region they visited.

Before we look at several fund-raising ideas, a word of caution. The fund-raiser can be a key means to help the church pay for the entire team without disturbing the general fund. But it may not be the most effective. Some churches ask for financial support from the congregation, then divide the total receipts by the number of mission trip participants. This may be democratic, but is it fair? Should the trips of those who do not need financial help be subsidized while reducing only slightly the cost for others who can barely afford it? It may be wiser to apportion the congregation's gift to those who have asked for scholarships.

Twenty Fund-raising Ideas

Many fund-raising events can involve fun, low-key yet competitive sports events, such as a golf tournament.[1] Also consider the following twenty fund-raising ideas:

1. Dinner a la Heart
2. Talent show
3. Church-wide yard sale
4. Trivial Pursuit marathon
5. Road rally
6. Mystery trip
7. Chili cook-off
8. Bake sale
9. Sell cookbooks
10. Craft fair
11. Square dance
12. Quilt raffle
13. Circus
14. Amusement fair
15. Pancake breakfast
16. Spaghetti dinner
17. Treasure hunt
18. Murder mystery
19. Gift-wrap table at mall or large store
20. Baby-sitting

. . . And Six More

Here are six other events, somewhat unusual in nature, that your church might consider sponsoring to raise funds for a short-term missions project:

1. *Jail-a-thon.* Volunteers show up at a jail cell you have installed in a popular local spot, such as a restaurant. Dressed in jail fatigues, they are given a telephone and directory and told to come up with bail money. During the typical two-hour stint, some of the conversations are quite amazing: "Joe, this is Pastor Pat. I'm calling from jail and need you to help bail me out." That usually gets people's attention. Then explain the purpose, of course, and take pledges, which your team then collects by mail, with a thank-you note and fuller explanation of where their pledge is going.

2. *Auction of donated goods and services.* Ask local merchants, restaurants, and members to donate products, services, and gift certificates that can be auctioned at a special gathering. A private plane ride followed by dinner sold for $250 at one event—and had three people wanting it at that price! Don't overlook youth: many of them will donate an evening's baby-sitting or a half-day of yard work, which together can contribute hundreds of dollars. Gift certificates at restaurants almost always sell for face value.

3. *Duck race.* Buy (or have someone donate, or have a sponsor buy) a bunch of yellow bathtub ducks. Carefully number each one, and "sell" them off. Buyers can even name their duck. On the appointed day, release the ducks into the creek together and

the first rubber ducky to cross the finish line wins! (Typically, a donated dinner at a nice restaurant makes a good prize.)

4. *Theater party.* A local semiprofessional theater will often offer a very low rate if you buy out the entire theater for one of their musical or dramatic shows. You can then make it "(Your group name) Night at the (XYZ) Theater" and charge the normal price.

5. *Car wash.* I know, a car wash sounds common, but . . . instead of the typical youth car wash, make it a professional job. Talk with a local car wash and ask them if they would give you, say, 30 percent of the face value if you sold tickets good for a month or two. They might want to exclude Saturdays, but then you have a much more salable product because you are not depending on a day's weather and attendance, and can sell more than one ticket to someone.

6. *Buy a brick.* People like to envision where their money is going. Asking for "money toward our trip," fails to create that clear vision. Suggesting $50 to buy ten bags of cement for the Habitat house, $200 for the front doors of the church you are building, or $100 to buy a calf that will supply the family with milk, lets donors feel their money is doing specific good and involves them mentally in your mission. In that way they can visualize buying the components to construct the building, almost like buying a brick.

Tips for Team Leaders

Habitat for Humanity, with affiliates in fifty countries, knows a thing or two about how its volunteer work teams can raise funds. Here is an excerpt from their tip sheet for team leaders on the subject. I am grateful to Habitat and John Yeatman of their Global Village Department for permission to pass on the advice, much of which can be adapted to your own project's needs:

Getting started

Very few people enjoy fund-raising and some are even downright intimidated by the thought of asking others for money. Nevertheless, do not worry—being a little uneasy with the idea is perfectly natural. Experiment with different approaches until you find one that is comfortable for you. Once you get into it, you will be surprised by how easy and fun it can be.

So now what?
Get psyched and try it! Here are a few tips to consider . . .

- Almost everyone you ask will support you; most people will give simply because you are asking!
- Be prepared, know how [the mission will] work and be prepared to answer questions; the more informed you are, the better your chance of getting sponsored.
- Start with people you know well; they will probably be open to what you are doing and want to support your efforts; then move onto anyone and everyone you can think of.
- If someone says "no" to your request, it is not a reflection on you.
- Many people make the mistake of not asking for a specific amount; people are most likely to give more if you offer categories (for example, $50, $100, $250) or average the cost per day (for example, @ $100/day, ask folks to sponsor a day or a half day). Don't try to decide how much you think they will be able to help—let them decide how much to pledge.
- Developing financial help from a network of supporters builds a base for those who will uplift you in their prayers for the work you are doing.[2]

Habitat for Humanity gives a lengthy list of people team members can ask for support. In addition to friends, family, and people at church, the agency recommends asking coworkers, people with whom you do business (some of whom would love to support a charitable outreach involving someone they know), service groups, men's fellowship groups, etc.[3]

Habitat for Humanity recommends three approaches to fund-raising, though it emphasizes that "personal contact is the key": (1) face-to-face, (2) a conversation on the telephone, and (3) having a mail campaign. Clearly, face-to-face would be the most effective of the three. But whether talking face-to-face or over the phone, "tell them they can help in one of two ways: they can come along with you or they can pledge money to send *you.*"

Similarly, if sending an appeal letter, "Do not forget to ask them to make a commitment or write a check and send it back to you as soon as possible. Include self-addressed envelopes, pre-stamped. Make it easy for them." Follow up your contacts with a call "to be sure they got your letter and answer any questions the mailing may have created."[4]

A sample fund-raising letter from Global Mission Fellowship concludes this chapter; it contains several of these elements.

Habitat for Humanity cites these four fund-raising commandments:

1. Thou shalt make it as easy as possible to give.
2. Thou shalt not allow fund-raising efforts to monopolize your time.
3. Thou shalt remember to be cost-effective.
4. Thou shalt always keep the big picture in mind.[5]

There is no right or wrong way to fund mission trips; each has certain advantages and drawbacks. Just be sure that whether a team member underwrites the entire trip herself, or twenty supporters each send in $100, always have all checks payable to the church. A check payable to individual participants is not tax deductible, even when it is to support their mission work.

TAKING MONEY WITH YOU

Team leaders should ask the mission specialist or host missionary how much additional money team members should take for out-of-pocket expenses. The leaders should also learn whether credit cards, ATM (automatic teller machine) cards, and travelers' checks are widely accepted in the host community. Do not assume they will be! Many less-developed countries (LDCs) do not accept credit cards and traveler's checks outside of the large cities.

You should also ask your host for advice on where to exchange money. Avoid asking over the telephone or by letter if you wish to exchange money "privately" with him. Although this is widely done, it is still illegal in many countries. Beware of street hustlers. They are easy to find, (actually, they will find you) and will greet you with a, "Psst! Wanna change dollars?" This practice is illegal—it is also a racket usually run by con artists. Stories abound of tourists who thought they got an extra few cents on the dollar, only to find the wad of bills they received had double-folded currency, or even blank pieces of paper, all through it.

Take several one-dollar bills with you. If you do have to tip a baggage handler or table server in a foreign country and have yet to exchange money, a twenty-dollar bill will not be much help! Here is a quick guide on the advantages and disadvantages of how to take your spending money.

Cash dollars are the easiest to exchange (although certainly don't bring hundred-dollar bills). Avoid taking bills that are torn or have writing on them, however. Banks in foreign countries often will not accept any bills not in mint condition. You can buy some foreign currencies from your hometown bank before you leave. The big disadvantage is you have no protection if you lose your money.

Credit cards are good for larger purchases in stores. They also give you full protection if the card is lost, provided you quickly report it. (Your maximum liability is only fifty dollars.) However, credit cards often are not accepted in rural areas and LDCs.

ATM cards give you quick access to cash when you need it (so you don't carry a lot on you at any one time and can have access in an emergency). ATM machines offer the best exchange rates, and they are now found in most large cities around the world, even in many overseas airports. Again, the disadvantage is machines and banks may not accept the card in your destination (they are generally not accepted in rural areas and LDCs), and you may need a new PIN number for international use. Overseas, these cash cards don't always seem reliable (I tried vainly for three days to use my card in Australia, then just as suddenly it worked again. In Hong Kong it refused to work the first two attempts, then immediately complied with my third request without hesitation).

Traveler's checks feature complete replacement if you lose them. For easier acceptance, try to buy them in the currency of your destination. Some institutions, such as credit unions and some auto clubs, waive the service charge. There are some financial disadvantages to buying them. There is often a service charge, and they are usually subject to higher exchange fees and a worse exchange rate than cash. Nor are they always accepted, especially in rural areas and LDCs.

When it comes to exchanging money for foreign currency, you should consult your missionary hosts for the best places. Generally, the following institutions reflect the order of best exchange rates: (1) ATM machines, (2) banks, (3) currency exchanges (often called *Bureaux De Change* overseas), (4) hotels and travel agencies, and (5) retail stores.

THE COLOR OF MONEY

The color of money sometimes is red. Many people, including husbands and wives, become angry or defensive when the subject is spending or finding money. Members of the mission team can begin to feel this way too. Short-term mission team leaders have heavy fiscal responsibilities.

As a team leader, be careful and deliberate during the planning stage. Think slowly through every event, every day, listing each activity that will cost money so that you can include it in your projections. Pay attention to interim payment due dates so you do not find something such as your flights canceled because you did not send in a timely payment. Follow the currency conversion tips in this chapter (if this is an international mission), and always add a "miscellaneous" amount for safety.

Be prepared to discuss fund-raising options with your team, but if possible, delegate the ultimate responsibility for raising their prorated trip cost to the participants. Include a "Fund-raising update" segment in each team meeting as you plan for the trip. Be scrupulous in the accounting of every penny coming in and out of the account, preferably by appointing a treasurer and some form of safety net such as vouchers or double signatures required for each expenditure.

SAMPLE GLOBAL MISSIONS FELLOWSHIP TEAM MEMBER FUND-RAISING LETTER[6]

Dear (name):
[Make first paragraph a personal greeting & introduction]

God has opened the door for me to go on a short-term mission trip to Panama with Global Missions Fellowship July 8–15, 19XX. We will be working with existing churches in the city of Colon, which are starting new baby churches there. I will be teamed up with one or more Panamanian Christians as we go door-to-door telling people about Jesus Christ through translators and bilingual literature.

Your help is needed! This is a team project, and you are needed on the team. First, we need your prayers for the spiritual battles ahead. Second, your help is needed to help cover part of the cost for this trip.

The total cost is $____. Please consider investing $____ or $____ in the project. Much of this amount is due by_____ .

If you would like to join us in this, please make your check payable to "Global Missions Fellowship," and return it to me in the enclosed envelope. GMF will then send you a tax receipt.

If I do not hear from you by _____, I will attempt to contact you to see what you have decided. I can answer any questions you may have at that time.

You are very important to me. Thank you for praying about being a part of our team.

Sincerely,

[Your name]

NOTES

1. Of course there will be a fee to enter the tournament. Other sports contests to consider are (1) a bridge tournament or marathon, (2) a basketball tournament, (3) a tennis tournament, (4) a celebrity golf/tennis outing, and (5) a ski trip. In addition, a walk-, run-, swim-, bike-, or bowl-a-thon, in which participants sign up sponsors to pledge so many dollars per mile (or games played), also keeps the athletes busy, happy, and contributing.
2. Elizabeth Earle, "Get Rolling . . . Build Your Support," booklet published by Habitat for Humanity (Americus, Ga, 1996), 1–3.
3. For other suggested contacts, see chapter 9 of William P. Dillon, *People Raising* (Chicago: Moody, 1993).
4. Earle, "Get Rolling," 4–5.
5. Ibid., 6.
6. © 1997, Global Missions Fellowship, Inc., of Dallas, Texas. Letter used by permission of Global Mission Fellowship with "attribution to the glory of our Lord and the advancement of His kingdom."

Chapter Six

✳

BUILDING YOUR MISSION TEAM

*"B*uilding Your Mission Team." All four words in this chapter title are worthy of reflection.

Building. The group of people selected for a short-term mission trip must work as a team to be effective. It takes time to mold your team into a cohesive unit. That is one reason you should start work on building your team about one year before the actual trip. It is vitally important to meet together often to prepare spiritually and mentally. With each meeting, personalities will develop, bonds will be forged, and a greater sense of purpose will result.

Your. Team leaders may have heard good news or horror stories about other mission groups. But if you are the group leader, this is *your* team. Even if you are not the team leader, as a participant who is heeding God's call to mission work, you also are following a sacred assignment, and you are part of a unique team. If you are leading the group, you have been issued a mandate by your church governing body as you direct this important ministry, representing Christ and a local body of believers. You have a greater opportunity than any other person to set the tone for their work together. Plan ahead, delegate responsibilities, remain calm and flexible, and act as a servant of the Lord and you will be ahead of the game as the molder of a productive, fun, effective team.

Mission. Never lose sight of the team's purpose. The objective is not to go and do good work. Neither is it to have the team members return home feeling good about themselves. Hopeful-ly, both of those conditions will occur, but a Boy Scout troop or Lions' Club can chase those aspirations. This is a team of servants of the Lord, disciples following Christ's direct instructions to take His gospel to the world, and to help people in need whom we meet on the journey.

Team. In the secular world, a group of star athletes, effective employees, or a crack military unit all find success for the same reason: They have woven their differing interests and back-grounds into a team. Numerous books have been written and cor-porate executives have spent millions of dollars to train people on the benefits that accrue to the organization that develops its employees into close-knit teams. The same holds true for mission groups. This is not a package tour. It is an adventure into unfa-miliar territory, where the culture, living conditions, and de-mands experienced by the participants can cause considerable stress. Members who work together as a team will succeed, as they look out for and support each other.

Vastly different outcomes have resulted from mission groups that traveled to the same destination and experienced the same conditions. The only difference was one group had followed the suggestion of meeting several times before departure, while the other groups did not. Those pre-trip meetings were used to em-phasize the importance of becoming a team. The other groups elected not to bother, figuring, as one group leader said, "There will be plenty of time to come together as a team when we get there." How well the group is already a team when they travel de-termines how the members deal with irritations such as the per-son who stays in the shower "too long," the individual who is always late, and so on. In chapter 8 you will find recommended agendas for up to ten team meetings.

ASSEMBLE A CORE GROUP

Have you ever hung a poster, or made an announcement heralding a great event—say, a fellowship outing to the theater—only to find the response is negligible? Then after you cancel the event, people tell you how it sounded like fun! Some people seem to have a fear about publicly signing up for such events, and so it is for mission trips. Many folks will think, "Hmm, sounds interesting. I wonder who else is going and what it costs. What could I do if I went?" When they see nobody else's name on the sign-up sheet on the bulletin board, they are even more hesitant to put their name on the list.

It works well to first select a core group, perhaps even before you publicly announce the trip. Over coffee, or away from the interruptions of a Sunday morning, tell these people of your idea. If you have maps, information on the host community, prices, etc., discuss those details. However, do not get too bogged down with secondary details. Your main objective is to share your vision and help them catch the dream, too. Be sure to provide paper for everyone to make notes, and encourage them to suggest ways to make the proposed mission even more effective.

Whom should you invite to the core group meeting? Many of them will probably be your friends, since we all tend to mix with people who share our own interests. Invite the following people:

- People who have some experience, perhaps having taken previous mission trips
- People whose advice and ideas you respect
- Members who can contribute to the success of the mission, financially or with their skills
- People who have lots of contacts that can be used to enlist participants, supplies, or financial support
- Church members whom the congregation respects

DETERMINE THE ACTIVITIES OF YOUR MISSION

From the core group meeting, you can probably determine the viability of the mission trip idea. The notes you took at that session should also give you an idea of the tasks your team can likely attempt. This is very important, because one of the first questions people will ask you is: "What can I do to help if I go on this trip?" Here is a tiny sampling of the kind of work often done by short-term mission teams:

- Teach Vacation Bible School
- Perform building construction/repair

- Activities with teenagers
- Evangelize/preach
- Lead adult Bible study
- Teach/provide medical care
- Teach local church leaders
- Minister/deliver supplies to poor/shut-ins
- Teach farmers, businesspeople, etc.
- Assist in church planting
- Teach English
- Lead women/men's Christian fellowship
- Reach out to outcast minorities (refugees, gypsies, Kurds, etc.)

By the time you have identified the tasks to be done, and confirmed with the on-site church or missionary that such assistance is needed and welcomed, it is time to start recruiting. You might convene another meeting of the core group to update them of the status. As they look over the list, ask them to match people who have some of the specific skills needed.

You will be amazed at how many names will be suggested—many of whom you probably did not previously know. "Joe Adams used to run our VBS for years, and his wife Sue is a doctor who specializes in pediatrics," is a typical type of response. Ask who will call each name suggested, and note those assignments for follow-up, if needed. You now have an excited, committed core group, a clear idea of what your team will do in the host community, and a list of qualified prospects who are about to be personally contacted by people they know and respect.

THE CAMPAIGN FOR PARTICIPANTS

Of course, you also want to invite other members from your congregation—all who would pray and sense God's leading—to participate in His short-term mission trip. Ask your pastor for time to make announcements during the worship services. Remember, when you speak, avoid boring statistics or lengthy readings from Scripture. Effective talks are those that touch emotions. People want to have a word picture painted in their minds of the reason for this trip. A message might have the repeated theme, "Let me tell you what a difference *you* can make to an orphaned child (elderly shut-in, new Christian family—or to whomever you will be ministering)." Mention the names of the core group people who have agreed to go—especially if they are well-known and respected. That makes the trip even more appealing to others.

Posters at church, handouts in the weekly bulletin and at adult Sunday school, announcements in the church newsletter: all are good vehicles for advertising the trip, and all should clearly promote the first meeting. Talk with church circles, youth groups, and other gatherings of members.

Those in sales and marketing at times practice "shotgun marketing," in which anyone and everyone hears the message; it is quite different from "target marketing," or the "rifle approach." The message described above was a classic shotgun approach. It was a general announcement saying, "Hey, everybody! We're running a mission trip and here are the details." The advantage to the shotgun approach is that you can reach many people with minimal effort. The disadvantage is that 90 percent of the people in the sanctuary at that moment may have no interest, no ability, or not be suitable candidates for your mission team.

That is where target marketing comes in. You have already asked your core group to identify good trip candidates. Now go one step further. Ask your pastor, your mission committee chair, your youth leaders, and your buildings and grounds chairman whom they think could contribute by participating. Show those leaders your tasks list. Are you planning to provide health care? Construction? Who are the doctors, nurses, dentists, carpenters, contractors in your congregation? Do not overlook mentioning those tasks during your congregational announcement: the listeners may think of friends and even neighbors who have skills and an interest in missions. In fact, many mission trip participants are not members of the sending church, but arc enlisted by siblings, neighbors, or friends who heard the call and passed it on to them.

THE KICK-OFF MEETING

Once you have identified a list of people whose skills match the tasks you will attempt, go to them individually and invite them to your kick-off meeting. Don't get into tireless logistics when you contact them. (Does it really matter what airline we are using?) Your objective is not to convince them to come on the trip, it is to sell them on the notion of a mission trip, and to persuade them to attend the meeting.

Set a date for the first meeting at least a month in advance. Avoid dates that conflict with church council, mission committee, choir, deacons, or such committees that might require attendance by your own interested parties. I also suggest not calling the first get-together the "first official team meeting." It sounds too intimidating. Try something like, "Initial Information Gathering," or "Mission Trip Q & A Fellowship."

During the crucial exploratory meeting, remember the adage, "Facts tell but stories sell." Paint a word picture of Christ's mandate for us to participate in missions, of the needs that exist in your target host community, and how each person can make a meaningful difference in addressing those needs.

The agenda might include (1) a Bible reading highlighting the scriptural call to missions, (2) a small informational packet describing the planned trip with printed materials on the needs, host country and community, estimated costs, etc., and (3) information on the mission agency or missionary host you are working with. The meeting should be primarily informational; you should not ask for deposit checks at the end of the gathering. Be sure to end the meeting by asking these prospective members to pray for God's will in establishing an effective, viable team during the period leading up to the group's formation.

The meeting differs from the first official team meeting (described in chapter 8) in that you are trying to assemble a core group of people who possess the skills you need and whom you believe can then be influential in persuading others to join the team when the mission trip is announced.

WHOM TO CHOOSE FOR THE TEAM
The Application Form

You should not automatically accept anybody who wants to go. Why not? Out of consideration for the applicant and the other team members. Ask each applicant for a written application (which asks their reasons for wanting to go). The application also contains a medical history section, where applicants can list allergies, blood type, and recent serious medical conditions. (See Form 1, "Application to Join the Short-Term Mission Team," in Appendix A.) As the team leader you have the absolute right—indeed, the obligation—to know this information, and to take those medical forms (in a sealed envelope, for privacy) with you on the trip in case of medical emergencies. With this data, you (perhaps after consulting a doctor) can decide whether the applicant would be wise to join this mission trip. Would you let someone who had cancer two years ago join the team to Nigeria? Sure. Should you let a hemophiliac join your team to Albania? No way—not until that country has a way of screening its blood supplies.

After reviewing the medical history and trip application forms, team leaders should take the time to interview each applicant. If you are nervous, make up a list of questions in advance. Ask open-ended questions, those that they cannot answer with a "Yes" or "No." Be direct. Questions such as these help you quickly discover a person's motives:

"Why do you want to join this mission team?"

"Would you tell me a little about your own journey of faith?"

"Where do you think you can make your greatest contribution to the team's work?"

"How would you feel about sharing a dormitory with six other team members?"

The objective is not to interrogate people. Instead, the interview is the first step on the road to ensuring that this troop of individuals from various backgrounds and interests will come together as a cohesive team of servants with a single vision.

The Importance Of Prayer

Christ spent hours in prayer before He decided which people He should pick as His disciples "One of those days Jesus went out to a mountainside to pray, and spent the night praying to God. When morning came, he called his disciples to him and chose twelve of them" (Luke 6:12–13).

Clearly, if Christ devoted many hours before He would choose His followers, those He would send out in mission for Himself, we too should pray earnestly and specifically for guidance in selecting members for our mission team.

What About "Outsiders?"

Although most of the team applicants will be from your church, you will probably have some who are not. Assuming you have anticipated this and have no problem with it, here are three questions to consider:

1. Are They Christians?

One team to Vietnam was composed of sixteen Pentecostal Christians and a doctor who had heard about the trip from a friend and had signed up because she thought she could use her skills to help needy folks. She was Jewish, a fact never discovered because the group had not held team meetings to prepare members for the trip. Almost from the moment the airplane took off, three church members clumsily and repeatedly attempted to convert her to Christianity.

After two days on site, the doctor tried to change her ticket to fly home, but was not allowed to do so because of the airfare restrictions. For the remaining ten days, she did her medical volunteer work and then avoided all contact with the team, eating in her room or at restaurants by herself. The last words exchanged were "Why don't you people leave me alone?" screamed at the three overzealous church members as they latched onto her on the bus ride to Hanoi Airport.

You must anticipate this question: Since we are a Christian church, will we accept nonbelievers on the mission trip? If that doctor volunteered her services to you, you must know if there are some groups where she would fit right in, and others with whom she should never be placed. Your integrity mandates that you advise such a person of the Christian makeup of your team, and the likely activities in which they will be engaged.

2. Are They Used To A Different Style Of Worship?

Mission planners need a certain sensitivity if they plan to include team members from another denomination. Experience has shown that most church members with varying worship traditions, such as Baptist, Congregational, Lutheran, Methodist, and Presbyterian, can join in worship and ministry with some give and take by all participants. When a few individuals join the missions team from a church having very different worship and prayer styles, such as Pentecostal or charismatic Christians, they tend to conform to the overall team's style and make for a harmonious group.

Keep in mind, though, that when a large block of team members come from two very different churches, you can anticipate extra preparation and training. One team had roughly half the people from a Methodist church and half from a Pentecostal church. An attitude of "us and them" occurred from almost the first moment. The two groups did not sit with members from the other denomination; after the workday, each group would assemble in their own private retreat for snacks and fellowship; and some members even discovered that one group was not attending the nightly team meeting because they were having their own "team" meeting! It got worse. When members of the charismatic group began praying aloud and speaking in tongues over an injured team member, some individuals from the other denomination started laughing.

How should team leaders address these problems? First, by being forewarned, you are already ahead of the game. Second, if you have two large blocks of Christians from two very different types of church, why not propose two separate mission trips? Third, if you do have to mix them together on one team, you need to stress even more the importance of each person accepting—and embracing—every one of their co-mission workers as vital components.

You also might ask the members of each church to alternate leading the spiritual time every evening. And if the team includes teenagers who have not been exposed to differing kinds of worship, you might talk with them privately *before* the trip takes place. Explain that they may encounter differing styles of prayer, but that it is as important for them to understand cultural differences within the mission team, too.

As with so many other issues, we can find our answer to these conflicts in Scripture. In Ephesians 4:1–6, Paul writes from prison to the church at Ephesus, acknowledging the differences in people's form of worship. But he reminds believers then and now that "There is one body and one Spirit, . . . one Lord, one faith, one baptism . . . " It is a beautiful passage that can be read together as a humbling, unifying message whenever you feel your team shows signs of divisiveness.

3. Will They Attend the Predeparture Meetings?

Those participating from outside your church may live a significant distance from your church. Whenever possible, they should attend the team meetings to prepare for the new culture and develop important team identity. If this is not feasible, they should be willing to get important materials and notes (or better yet, a recording of the meetings). Strategies for doing this are detailed in chapter 8 (see "Mandatory Attendance?").

What About Age?

People frequently ask: "Do you think she is too young (or too old) to go on the trip?" There can be no simple answer. Mission teams have included ten-year-olds and octogenarians. A twelve- or thirteen-year-old is probably as young as you would want on an overseas trip to a developing country, in part because a child any younger than that will require parental supervision that detracts from the adult's effectiveness. Realize, also, that the typical child of that age is often loathe to try new foods.

You should really put the question directly to the escorting family member: "Here is the situation. There will be no television, no toys, no air-conditioning, no McDonald's. Why does the child want to go? Every member of this team is going because they have a specific skill they will be contributing. What contribution do you think this child can make to the overall team objective?"

An adolescent can make a great addition to a team planning to work with children in the host community. We insist on bringing teens on trips where our on-site work includes youth ministry. Several senior citizens who participated on other mission trips were able to hold Bible study meetings with elderly local residents that evolved into wonderfully effective, deeply appreciated experiences and lasting relationships.

On the other hand, the immature youth who lacks the social skills to be a full member in the team of adults can wreck the trip. So can anyone who has not been adequately prepared for the conditions on your mission into third-world conditions.

DIFFICULT PEOPLE

Team leaders must be prepared to deal with difficult people, whatever their age. In chapter 8, I outline agendas for ten pre-trip meetings. Holding eight to ten meetings before departure has many benefits, and a key one is that you can see personalities developing before the group is thrown together in the stresses of another cultural setting. From the very first gathering, establishing the team leader's authority is important—not for the sake of power, but because the group must accept the team leader as having the last word on operational and logistical decisions. A covenant signed by each participant (see Form 2 in Appendix A) shows that rule when they first enroll.

What do you do about the teen who consistently shows up at team meetings having failed to do the assigned preparation work? Or the "know-it-all" who continually interrupts you to add their opinions? Or the member who misses three out of every four team meetings? Before taking overt action, try reading James 1:19. He admonishes us to be "quick to listen," (the better to try to understand all points of view); "slow to speak," (setting the tone as wise leaders who only talk after careful deliberation); and "slow to anger; for your anger does not produce God's righteousness" (NRSV).

The first step is to determine whether the situation requires action. If left to continue, does it just unnerve you a little, or could it affect the mission trip's effectiveness? If it could threaten the team's effectiveness, the next step is to talk with the individual privately.

Before you open your mouth, conduct what Zig Ziglar calls "A check up from the neck up." Check your own attitude. The proper mind-set for the meeting should be "How can we resolve this?" rather than "Who is to blame?" Can you objectively define the problem? One test is to try writing the problem down, then read it back to yourself to see if it makes sense.

Try to assess the reason for the person's behavior. Is it childish immaturity? Does the individual resent having someone so much younger at the helm? Is he a world traveler, trying to impress the group? Be specific. Be brief. Having stepped into their shoes to see why they caused the stir, explain that they need to see things through your eyes: the task of organizing a mission team is complex, time-consuming, and frustrating enough that there can be no room for disruptive people. Explain that you want them to participate, that they can make a real difference to the people in the host community, but that it is incumbent on every member to fulfill his responsibilities.

Conflict resolution specialists caution against using "you" language. Avoid putting your case in extreme terms, such as "always" and "never." Saying "You are always late" will probably be perceived as much more confrontational than "I can understand the time pressures each team member has, but the rest of the team considers our meeting time to be important enough to be on time." When I teach my interpersonal skills seminar, the class discovers through role-playing that they can get beyond the confrontational stage by using the Behavior-Consequence-Feeling-Action formula. You would say, in a very level, non-accusatory tone: "John, when you make one of your jokes while I am speaking to the group (behavior), everybody's concentration is broken (consequence), and I (we all) feel frustrated and even angry (feeling)." You could add the action step after a slight pause: "What I'm asking is that you respect everybody's position and keep your humor until the coffee break"(action).

There are times, however, when these or other techniques do not change the attitude or behavior. Even the best baseball hitter strikes out. This is one of those moments when team members are glad they do not have the responsibility for leading the group! Using your Christian values as a guide, you must honestly answer the question: "Will they jeopardize the work, fellowship, or effectiveness of the team if this person goes on the trip?" If the answer is anything other than a resounding "No!" then you must tell them they cannot participate.

Tough as that decision may be, acting now is infinitely better than to have to realize during the trip that you should have so acted. Ask any youth leader who has had to call a parent to come pick up their errant child in the midst of a summer camp, or the mission team leader who has driven a difficult person to the airport halfway through the trip: such incidents are so disruptive to the entire trip you will thank yourself for having the tenacity to act on your well-thought-out hunches before you leave home.

WHAT SIZE SHOULD THE GROUP BE?

How large or small should your team be? There is no right answer for all mission trips. A church might easily fill a school bus with forty teens on a youth mission to Appalachia. Yet forty people on a short-term mission to many small communities in LDCs (less-developed countries) would be too many. You must be careful not to overtax the resources of the local mission host. Generally, teams of between twelve and twenty people tend to be the ideal size. Much fewer than that and you cannot earn group discounts and the pro rata costs go up; much larger and you spend all your time taking care of logistics.

THE STRONG MISSION TEAM

There is no challenge more important to mission team leaders than picking the right people for their crew. A group that negotiated the best rates and provided a superb on-site program can fall apart if a couple of the participants incessantly argue or complain. Conversely, a team that is Christ-inspired, well-chosen, and properly trained can see the best-laid preparations come undone and still have fun as they make great things happen for the people they came to serve.

The team leader needs to think ahead and plan accordingly. First, what do you want to accomplish on this mission? Now find people who possess those skills. Next, broadcast the news that there will be a mission work team to attract interest; then talk with each applicant to ensure everyone is on the same wavelength and driven by the same motivation. Finally, decide in advance how you want to handle nonmembers of your church and clearly define the behavioral expectations; be prepared to honestly deal with interpersonal problems that could adversely affect the team.

If you are a member of a short-term mission group, you should understand that the leader needs your prayers and support. Chances are he or she is an unpaid volunteer who has taken on the awesome task of bringing a group of excited strangers into a foreign environment where they are thrown together with cultures, languages, and personalities all clashing simultaneously. This is not a guided tour. It is a Christian mission trip, and the more you can support your team leader the more you also are demonstrating your own humility and discipleship.

If you are the team leader, do not be daunted by the challenges. Remember, you are following in the footsteps of Jesus Christ Himself—who was also charged with the responsibility of building an effective team. He knew He would be confronted with attitudes and behavior that would require His attention. Even the twelve apostles had personality clashes. But like the Master, you can mold a team that wants to honor God in their service.

Chapter Seven

※

MAKING TRAVEL ARRANGEMENTS

*M*ost short-term mission trips will take team members into a different culture, and typically this means another country. Unless you are traveling somewhere in the United States or just across the border into Mexico—where a church or charter bus is the carrier—this also means airline travel. And it's up to the team leader to make the travel arrangements.

You have done your homework and you are ready to operate a mission work trip. For the sake of this example, let us say you are going to São Paulo, Brazil, to help a local missionary's outreach to abandoned street children, and you plan to take thirty people. You have four options on whom to call: (1) a local travel agent, (2) an airline, (3) a consolidator, or (4) a missions specialist. Let's look at the advantages and limitations of each resource in arranging your travel.

THE TRAVEL AGENT

A travel agent can be your best friend or your worst nightmare. The problem is, you probably will not know into which category your agent falls until the trip is under way. There is no licensing nor even required training for travel agents. Remember, the agent who booked your neighbors to Disney World and has been on a dozen cruise ships may know less than you about remote foreign destinations. I have seen travel agents bluff their way through complex itineraries; witnessed occasions when they did not tell the passenger she needed a visa to enter a foreign country;

I have seen them make hotel arrangements in Fayetteville, North Carolina when the air tickets were to Fayetteville, Arkansas!

Clearly, their expertise, efficiency, and experience can vary from agency to agency. By all means, ask around for recommendations of travel agents who have successfully handled your type of arrangements before. Then interview them. See if they appear too anxious to book you on only one airline—often a sign of kickbacks called "override commissions"—and an indication of where their loyalties lie. If you are satisfied and confident, go ahead and deal with them. However, never forget, you are the ultimate responsible party. Always ask questions, and on important matters, like visas, double-check their answers with another reliable source, such as an embassy.

A good travel agent is a great resource. If you find one, hang onto him—and tell all your friends! Agents earn commission from travel providers, such as airlines and hotels, so their service does not cost you a dime. The more business they generate, the more revenue for the agency, so a good agent will appreciate any referrals. Agents are usually local—you might even have one in your congregation—so the personal touch is much more likely to be present than if you deal directly with an airline.

A travel agent can also help you find space on a charter airline. Charters can save you money, but be aware of the risks involved. Charters historically tend to have a less reliable on-time record, generally have more cramped seating, and may be canceled if they do not fill up. If a cancellation occurs shortly before your departure, you may find all the cheaper advance-purchase seats on scheduled airlines sold out. Finally, should a charter airline go out of business, passengers are not afforded the protection offered by scheduled carriers, especially having other airlines accepting their tickets to carry you home. And because you cannot usually pay for charters with a credit card, if a charter carrier closes its doors after you've paid, you probably will have little recourse in getting your money back.

THE AIRLINE

You can book directly with an airline, too. To find out which airlines fly to your destination, check the *Official Airline Guide* (OAG) or the electronic services such as EasySaabre, American Express, or Preview Travel found on most computer systems. America Online, CompuServe and Prodigy all have travel reservations linkups, and if you are not a subscriber, try your local library.

They usually list nonstop flights first. So-called "direct" flights are not nonstop; they make one or more en route stops but you need not change planes. Connecting flights are shown after nonstop and direct services. Beware of the newly popular "code shared flights," which show one flight number from, say, Milwaukee to London. Only when you board do you realize that airline A will fly you to Boston, then you have you change to airline B. It is misleading (and unethical in my opinion) and can be distressing to the inexperienced traveler who thinks she is getting a nonstop flight on airline A.

Be flexible when considering airlines. If you live in Grand Rapids, for example, you might find a much better selection of carriers and rates out of Chicago. In the airline business, more competition usually means lower prices. For instance, you have a wide variety of flights and fares flying from major international airports to São Paulo; you can fly on American, Continental, United, TransBrasil, or Varig Brazilian Airlines.

The next step is to call the airlines' toll-free numbers and ask for the group desk. Tell them what you are planning and that you are shopping for the best fare between their competitors and they will give you a rate. One recent exercise resulted in three airlines quoting group fares of $580, $700 and $810 per person for the same itinerary. When informed of the lower fare, the higher carriers dropped their quotation to $580 and $600!

Think ahead: Will you have special requirements, such as ten extra bags full of medical supplies? What if 20 percent of your team is coming home a week after the others, yet the fare rules limit such deviations to 10 percent? This is the time to negotiate those little extras. Especially when you share with the airline the nature of your trip, most carriers tend to be extremely helpful. For example, I took thirty-seven cartons of toys to our new orphanage in the Dominican Republic; 2,000 pounds of medical supplies to Beirut; and extra bags on each of eleven Romania mission trips, without ever having to pay a penny in excess baggage charges.

When the group desk quotes the fare, make sure you ask about:

- Taxes, "facility charges," and security fees. Are they included, both in the U.S. and overseas? Nowadays such charges can add $40 or more per ticket.
- Confirmation. Are they confirming your block of seats at this rate?
- When (and how much) do you need to send as a deposit? When is the balance due?
- What is the minimum number of passengers you must pay for to get this rate?
- When must they have your group's names?
- If an individual cancels at the last minute, will they let you substitute a replacement?
- Do you have any deviations from the group (flying out a day early, etc.)?

The cheapest airfare is not always the best. A $50 lower fare was not so attractive to an Atlanta team when they realized they had to fly from Birmingham, Alabama—a two-and-one-half-hour bus ride each way—compared to nonstop service from Atlanta. In 1996, a mission team traveled from New York to Budapest, Hungary. Airline A's fare was $40 less than airline B's, but they wanted full payment four and one-half months earlier than B, and would not permit any name changes after that date. Knowing that mission teams frequently have changes in the four months before the departure, and that each member would not have their money raised by March for an August trip, the team leader concluded airline B had the better deal. Another team could have saved a few dollars on their airfare by flying from Philadelphia to Kiev via Detroit and Amsterdam. However, the routing meant six more hours in layovers and travel time than the next-most-expensive airline's routing. Was a $30 per-person savings worth six hours longer in airports and airplanes?

THE CONSOLIDATOR

In the bad old days of airline regulation, you could save a lot of money by buying your tickets at a "bucket shop." Usually located in dark alleys of large cities, it seemed like you were dabbling in espionage. If you knocked three times and said the secret word, someone would sell you a ticket, say from London to Nairobi at one quarter the regular fare. One group I know did exactly that. They had to go via Moscow, Cairo, and Entebbe to reach Nairobi, but what a bargain!

Today, discounts are legal and the biggest reductions are often found through consolidators. They can offer their bargain rates because they take blocks of seats on certain carriers year-round. They also help fill airplanes of carriers who have little exposure in a market: would *you* think of Singapore Airlines between New York and Frankfurt, Japan Airlines from Los Angeles to Rio de Janeiro, or Kuwait Airways from Chicago to Amsterdam? You can see their ads in the travel or classified sections of large metropolitan newspapers like the *New York Times,* especially the Sunday editions. They have even made inroads onto Main Street with some local travel agents using them for special clients.

Consolidators offer great prices—often as much as 50 percent off the fares—but no advice. They are not travel agents. They will not try to get some free bags negotiated with the airline for you. They usually require full payment at the time of booking, may charge extra for credit card payment, and even if they put you on your favorite airline, the tickets may not earn frequent flyer miles (so ask in advance). The best discounts are usually on the more expensive tickets, especially to destinations in Asia and Africa. The most popular destinations, such as Europe in the summer, and the most highly regarded airlines, such as Singapore Airlines and Swissair, usually offer fewer discounts.

Some consolidators sell directly to the public, others only deal with travel agents, who add a commission—typically 10 to 12 percent—and resell the ticket to you.

THE INDEPENDENT MISSION SPECIALIST

This is a position created out of necessity because so many churches and team leaders lack the time and experience to pull everything together themselves. A mission specialist will consult with you to learn your needs, arrange all the travel details—even the mission destination if you want—provide guidance from the kickoff team recruitment presentation to the point of escorting the group if you require. There are not many of us around, so the best way to find one is to ask other leaders in the missions department of your denomination or a local Bible college.

PASSPORTS AND VISAS

Except for a few nearby nations such as Bermuda and some Caribbean countries, which only require proof of U.S. citizenship, all travelers will need a passport for international travel. Particularly if your mission trip is during the summer, team members should apply for their passport well in advance—allowing two months is a minimum. Team leaders should ask each person to check his or her existing passport to ensure it is still current. U.S. passports remain valid for ten years after their issue.

Photocopies of birth certificates are not acceptable, so the lengthiest part of the application process is often the time it takes to gather the required documentation. The "Certified Copy" of your birth certificate required for a new passport (and some visas) does not mean a photocopy signed by a notary public. Neither will the hospital birth certificate suffice. Only certified copies with a raised seal from the state of your birth (usually the department of health or vital statistics) is acceptable. Replacements for expired passports can be applied for using the old passport as proof of birth.

Passport information can be obtained both by mail and computer. An excellent booklet, "Passports: Applying for Them the Easy Way" is available for fifty cents from the Consumer Information Center, Department 356A, Pueblo, CO 81009 at 719-948-3334, along with passport application forms for those who need them. Passport applications can be distributed at the second team meeting. Application forms for both new and replacement passports also are available from the Internet. They can be downloaded from the U.S. State Department's World Wide Web site at http://www.state.gov. Team leaders should check to see that every team member has a U.S. passport.

A passport is the U.S. government's permission to travel outside America and to return; a visa is permission from the host country to visit. Many countries will accept a passport for entry— no visa is required; others require a visa only if you are planning to stay more than a few weeks or are working. But some nations require a visa even if you are staying only one day. Much depends on the country's relationship with the United States. And some countries who have good diplomatic relations still require you pay for a visa, which becomes a revenue-generating resource. In addition, a host country that requires no visa of U.S. citizens may require them from nationals of that third country, so a team member who is not a U.S. citizen may need a visa for entry.

How do you find out what the visa policies are for specific countries? Contact the U.S. State Department at 202-647-6225 (or its Internet website at http://www.state.gov) for the latest visa requirements. Many countries have relaxed their visa requirements in recent years, but you should not assume your destination country has. Team leaders should know before departure whether the host country requires a visa. The frontier—at midnight on a weekend—is no place to make that discovery!

A partial list of local U.S. passport agency offices is provided in Appendix F. If you do have an emergency need for a last-minute passport, the closest U.S. passport agency can usually accommodate you—for a higher fee. So can a private passport expediting service, again for a fee of usually between $35 and $70 *above* the passport charges.

If you do need visas, before you write "Christian Mission" on the visa applications, make absolutely sure the host country permits such activities to be conducted by visitors. Stating "Christian evangelism" as the reason for your application to visit Afghanistan, Saudi Arabia, Iran, or China (and many other countries) will definitely mean a denied entry. The rejection may come after you have sent a nonrefundable deposit to the airline; or you and the other team members may slip through, only to be turned around at your destination—after flying halfway across the world. Also, check to see if the visa-issuing nation requires one or two clean (stamp-free) pages on your passport, or a validity at least six months *after* your travel dates. Many Arabian countries will not honor your passport if it contains evidence that you traveled to Israel.

IMPORTANT DETAILS

As the team leader, overseeing and motivating a group of perhaps twelve or thirty individuals, you will care for lots of details. In the next chapter we will consider the details of your pre-departure meetings. First, however, let's look at the many details of organizing the trip that seem minor, yet are very important. They're easy to forget, but crucial to remember.

Getting the Dates Right

Travel dates are important; they can save you money (when traveling during an airlines' off-peak season or days) and can mean a hearty welcome from an overtaxed host missionary or pastor if you arrive at the right time. But when planning a trip, how you list your dates can lead to trouble when corresponding with an overseas vendor. Most of the world outside the United States writes dates in the day/month/year format, just as the U.S. military has practiced for years. So September 3, 1998 is actually 3 September 1998, and is written 3/9/98 (or 03/09/98), whereas in the U.S. we write it 9/3/98. Now imagine the implications for the group leader who makes reservations and sends nonrefundable deposits to travel suppliers for a trip on 9/3/98. You think you just paid for the team's bus and hotel arrangements for their arrival on September 3. Then on March 9 you get an international call from the bus company saying their bus and driver waited at the airport for you and you no-showed. The hotel faxes you, saying your prepaid, guaranteed rooms have been forfeited.

This sad, costly mistake occurred all because you followed your habit of writing the month first, while the overseas vendor wrote the day first. Always write out the dates fully when communicating internationally: September 3, 1998 would have avoided this dilemma.

One Parent Traveling With A Minor Child

In some countries entry may be denied an adult traveling with a minor child, even if it is a parent. This even applies to neighboring countries such as Canada and Mexico. Their concern over the possible abduction of the child (for instance, after an unfavorable custody ruling during a divorce) is admirable. If only one parent is with the child, an authorization may be needed. Be sure to check in advance with consular officials of all countries through which such family units will travel, and carry in the accompanying parent's possession a signed, notarized, sealed document in which the absent parent has given his or her permission for the traveling parent to escort the child.

A related situation is a child under age eighteen traveling on your team without either parent. In that scenario, the team leader should have written papers (preferably notarized) that give both parents' permission for their child to travel with the team. The signed document should be as specific as possible, giving the dates, flight routing, and the name of an adult who is responsible for the youth team member.

Obtaining an International Driver's License

If you plan to drive in a foreign country, do you need an International Driving License? It is really a misnomer, there is no test which then qualifies you for international driving conditions. It is simply a document in several languages with a photograph, and must be used in conjunction with your regular driving license. Most European and Caribbean countries no longer require an International License, but check with a local office of the American Automobile Association (AAA). If you do need one, they can issue one immediately for a charge of between $11 and $16.

Transporting Medical Supplies

What if you are taking a large quantity of prescription drugs into another country? Think through the moment of your arrival at the customs hall in your destination country, when the nice officer discovers twenty cartons of syringes and pills in your team's luggage. You tell him of your mission; in the movies, this is the part where the guy says, "*Vere are your papers?*" What will *you* give him? By thinking this out in advance, you can get a letter from a donating doctor or hospital stating the source of the medications, and a letter on church stationery verifying your mission.

A few weeks before you leave home, call the host country's embassy here in America and request they prepare a letter, written in their language, explaining the purpose of your visit. It should include a statement such as, "These people are coming to our country to help our citizens. We know they'll be bringing in medical supplies and do not bother them."

In addition, ask your U .S. representative and U.S. senator each to write a letter that says something like: "To whom it may concern. This is to introduce Mr. ABC and a team of people from

XYZ Church. They are visiting (name of country) on a humanitarian visit to take donated medical supplies to help the citizens of that nation. Please allow them to pass freely, without hindrance, and afford them any assistance that may be necessary." Of course, Senator So-and-so has no jurisdiction whatever in a foreign country. Nevertheless, my experience has been that when I took a polite but firm proactive stand, producing two or three documents, some of which have a very impressive gold seal and "United States Senate" at the top, no bureaucrat I have ever encountered has refused to let us pass, nor confiscated anything nor charged duty.

Pre-trip Immunizations

Government health agencies and departments often recommend vaccination against certain illnesses when traveling abroad. This is particularly true if your missions team will be working outside a major urban center. For immunization inquiries or details of any warnings on foreign health conditions, call the Centers for Disease Control (CDC) at 404-639-2572. If you have access to the Internet, another excellent resource for health warnings, entry requirements, and country profiles is Travel Health Online, reached through their website http://www.tripprep.com.

The immunization guidelines that follow should be used as an introductory aid only. Be sure to seek the advice of a qualified physician for preventive measures before venturing into areas where such diseases exist.

Cholera. The cholera vaccine is recommended during travel to affected areas and occasionally mandated for entry into certain countries. The vaccine is effective for only six months, so should be taken close to departure time. Not recommended for pregnant women.

Hepatitis A. Hepatitis A is one of the most common illnesses contracted by travelers. Immunization can prevent it, using the more traditional gammaglobulin or the newer Havrix vaccine. Havrix is a two-injection series which is said to provide ten-year immunity. It should be administered three weeks before travel into affected areas. Gammaglobulin, however, should be taken as close as possible to the travel date.

Hepatitis B. Immunization against hepatitis B requires a six-to eight-month course of vaccinations. Hepatitis B is an often-fatal disease, spread through sexual contact and through the blood and body fluids of infected persons. Although very common in many countries, it can be avoided by using the same cautions as used in America: avoid unsterilized medical and dental equipment, untested blood supplies, shared needles and razors, and unprotected sex.

Diphtheria. The U.S. government strongly recommends protection against diphtheria. A booster shot is needed every ten years.

Polio. Polio still infects an estimated half-million people each year in developing nations. This easily transmitted disease is still prevalent in Africa and India. Following childhood vaccinations, a booster every ten years is required to stay protected.

Smallpox. Smallpox has been exterminated globally. Immunization is no longer required.

Tetanus. Protection against tetanus is still highly recommended. If you have not had a booster shot within the past ten years, get one.

Meningitis. Meningococcal meningitis is an awful malady that has surfaced in parts of central Africa, Saudi Arabia, Nepal, and Mongolia. It can be prevented with a single vaccination.

Typhoid. Protection against typhoid lasts from only one to three years, so maintain a careful record of prior inoculations before venturing into affected areas. Typically, tropical or semitropical countries or environments where you might encounter contaminated food and water and raw sewage are at risk for typhoid. The traditional inoculations that caused some side effects (a little pain, occasional fever and cramps) have now been supplanted by a single-dose injectable vaccine with fewer side effects. This single-dose inoculation protects you for three years. There is also an oral form of typhoid vaccine.

Influenza. A flu shot against the latest strain is suggested for travelers over sixty-five or those who suffer from heart disease or chronic pulmonary problems.

Yellow Fever. Protection against yellow fever lasts for ten years and is especially recommended before travel to endemic areas in Africa and South America. Vaccination is not recommended during pregnancy.

Encephalitis. Japanese encephalitis, spread by mosquitoes, is an epidemic in certain areas of Asia, such as China, Thailand, India, Nepal, and Korea. (Ironically, the disease is no longer a problem in Japan.) The vaccine is administered in a series of three shots. Tick-borne encephalitis has been reported in growing numbers in Central Europe and the former Soviet Union. The series of three shots, administered over a six-month period, should be considered before embarking on trips where you might be camping or spending time where ticks are normally prevalent.

Remember, there is often a long lead time before the antibody becomes effective. Some vaccine treatments need to be started seven months before you leave home. Other vaccines may need to be ordered, or even administered in Europe en route to your destination because they are not available in the United States. The key to the successful short-term missions is advance planning. But now we're talking about your life. Plan ahead. Don't wait until the week before you leave before you call your doctor for protection. And even with the vaccination, you should still exercise the normal health cautions while onsite, such as using mosquito repellent, avoiding high-risk food and water, and staying away from raw meat and fish.

Insurance Needs

As the mission leader planning the trip, you should constantly stop and ask yourself, "What if . . .?"

What if . . . Two days before your mission team departs, the father of one of the participants dies. Can you get him his money back?

What if . . . To save money for your youth group's upcoming summer mission trip to Mexico, you get approval to travel there in the church bus. After the group arrives in Mexico, the bus is struck by a car. Will you be covered for liability, injuries, and repairs?

What if . . . During a mission project in Albania, a team member suffers a heart attack. Conditions in the local hospital are archaic. They do not screen their blood supply and even reuse sutures, yet to medevac the patient to a modern hospital in Vienna or Rome will cost $26,000. What can you do?

The answers to all these questions can be found in one word:

insurance. Address those questions before leaving home and you can avoid legal, medical, and emotional trauma later. The example of the church bus obviously warrants a call to your insurance broker to see if a rider or supplemental policy is needed for driving in Mexico. Incidentally, if you are renting a vehicle and use a gold credit card, the card company usually covers your collision damage waiver—often a $15–20 per day saving. Call and check before you leave home. Take care to ensure that the coverage is still effective should you leave a paved road. That may conflict with your need to drive up dirt tracks and along riverbeds to reach remote mission destinations.

You can buy travel insurance that covers lost baggage, trip cancellation costs because of a family member's sickness or death, and emergency medical care during the trip. There are many different companies and a wide range of rates. The toll-free telephone numbers of several major travel insurers are listed in Appendix F. (No endorsement is implied). Check the exclusions carefully. When I lead a team to a country where I would not feel confident being hospitalized (Romania, the former Soviet Union, much of Africa, for example), I make trip insurance mandatory for team members. Your inclusion of the premium in the package price is often best.

TROUBLESHOOTING BEFORE YOU GO

Uniglobe Travel of Vancouver, British Columbia, one of North America's largest travel agencies with more than 1,100 franchised offices, maintains a customer service hotline for clients in trouble. In a 1997 press release, Connie Smith, manager of the company's Rescue Line, reported on the most frequent problems encountered during the 140,000 annual calls that come in from Uniglobe's worldwide travel customers. The most recurrent complaint is from travelers who got the time, date, or flight number wrong and missed the flight. The second-largest number of calls arose from clients' packing essentials (medications, passports, eyeglasses, etc.) in checked baggage, when they should have been kept in their carry-on luggage. Those are good warnings to remember as you prepare for your short-term missions trip. Other common problems Uniglobe found from its international travelers that you can prepare for were:

- Arguing with the airline, hotel, rental car company, or a similar provider, worsening the problem. [There is a point when travelers cross the line from strongly making their case, to where they are so rude and obnoxious that the service provider just wants them out of his office.]
- Failing to read stopover rules on tickets. [If you are ticketed on a through fare from Houston to Cairo, just because you may change planes in Paris does not give you the right to spend a day or two there.]
- Assuming an advance-boarding pass, issued by the travel agency, guarantees the passenger a seat. [You still must present yourself at the gate within certain time limits. Wait until the last minute, and they can give away your seat.]
- Ignoring car rental restrictions. [There are minimum and maximum age requirements for car rental companies, and it is almost impossible to rent a car without using a valid major credit card issued in the renter's name.]
- Failing to produce the hotel's confirmation number.

Travel is a fascinating subject to many people. They think of a long flight across the ocean as exciting, romantic, adventurous. But be sure to plan for it. Then defer all questions about travel logistics, such as type of aircraft, meals being served, and preparing for jet lag, until the final team meeting. Instead, focus on the truly important issues: why you are going, what you can do to make a difference, learning the language, and so on.

Godspeed!

Chapter Eight

✵

PREPARING FOR THE TRIP

*W*herever you go and whatever you do, you need to prepare in order to be effective. If you are a golfer and were planning a trip to Scotland to play that country's finest courses, you would spend months practicing. If you like to explore and were joining others from your college alma mater on their summer archeological expedition, you would explore the Internet, the library, and every other source of information so that you were truly prepared before you departed home. So it is with mission trips. During your adventure, you will be an ambassador for Christ in a different culture. Are you sufficiently prepared that you could share your testimony in ways that are meaningful and will not cause offense to the host audience? Will you be able to participate and contribute in such a way that you both enjoy yourself and honor the Lord you serve?

Whether you are a team member embarking on a "once in a lifetime" experience or a team leader on your umpteenth mission trip, it is essential that you prepare for the right spiritual mindset. In addition, you must accept that you are part of a *team* and learn much about the cultural differences of the host community. Only in this way can each member contribute to the success of the team's total mission effort. In chapters 8 and 9 we will look at how to enhance team unity, prepare spiritually, and prepare for entering a different culture.

As the team leader, your advance work means every participant knows what is required. By now, team members should know where they are going, what kind of work the team will do when onsite, and what the trip will cost. As the leader, you also should know whether people need passports, visas, and special immunizations.

After all this groundwork, it's time for preparing the team members through a series of meetings. Months before the actual meetings, leaders should list the team meetings and draw up a working agenda. It is much easier to "see" the entire project that way, and adding some emerging issue into a meeting at the last minute is easy.

TEAM MEETINGS

The Objectives of Meetings

The secret to successful mission trips is preparation and training of the participants; the key to that preparation lies in the team meetings convened in the months leading up to the trip.

How many meetings does the team need before their departure? There is no hard rule about how many meetings or how frequently they should occur. Figure on holding at least eight, but no more than twelve. The meetings have four objectives. The group members need to:

- Build team camaraderie and morale.
- Enhance their biblical understanding of mission work.
- Develop their language skills (if appropriate) and cultural understanding of the host community.
- Prepare for the physical skills and logistical arrangements required for the trip.

Mandatory Attendance?

Attendance at every meeting should be mandatory. The problem is, you have to be careful about using words like "mandatory" when dealing with volunteers. If your pastor missed a meeting to deal with a counseling crisis, do you throw him off the trip? Of course not. So how would you respond to the nurse whose shift work schedule prevents her from attending a couple of team meetings?

Clearly, you cannot require compulsory attendance. But at

the first meeting you can remind them of the importance of attendance. During that meeting explain that you wish you had the power to command compulsory attendance. Then indicate your understanding and compassion. For instance, you might say, "I recognize our group includes many busy people. On occasion you may have to miss a meeting because of a more urgent need. If that happens, don't feel that you 'blew it.' Of course, try to come to every meeting. If you must miss one, just be sure to take personal responsibility for learning the material covered at each meeting." Make it clear that as the leader you do not have the time to sit down again and brief another person on the same things the rest of the team learned two nights earlier.

If you are a team member, you should have the same commitment to these meetings as your leader does. If you cannot attend a particular meeting, arrange with another team member to take notes or tape the meeting. (Some leaders choose to prepare audio and video recordings of each meeting.) If you are joining a mission team from another church and miss some meetings because of distance, be sure to have a fellow member mail an audio tape. This type of cooperation also serves the first objective of team meetings: It encourages you and your fellow members to work together as a team, helping each other as you prepare for the mission.

As a leader, be sure to talk early with a member who has joined the team from far away, being invited by a family member or friend. Be frank with the person, explaining the need for the team to know one other well by the time the trip takes place. Call for his or her commitment; without it, an "out-of-towner" may not help the team.

Three Women: Nora, Annie, and Debbie

An out-of-towner can actually hinder the team. I remember Nora (not her real name), who once had belonged to the church that was sponsoring a mission team to Kenya. After her parents divorced, Nora moved in with her father in West Virginia. For ten months, Nora had not made it to a single team meeting at the church in Philadelphia. The day the team left, she knew only three members of the team, had studied none of the notes nor completed any of the assignments the rest of the group had been working through. Nora's flight from West Virginia arrived just in time for her to be introduced to the other team members before their international flight departed. Because the rest of the team had checked in as a group, their seats were assigned in a different section from Nora's.

When the group arrived in Nairobi, nobody ran over and asked Nora to sit with them on the bus to the host community. They were not being hostile, it was just fact that by now they had formed alliances and friendships through the team-building exercises at the meetings.

Over the first day or so, the lonely Nora had wanted to latch onto two young people of her age but they were already best friends who regarded the stranger as a "third wheel."

Among the people, Nora showed little sensitivity, having missed the group's endless cultural sensitivity training during its team meetings. While with the local teens, she would flash her substantial spending money around, using such phrases as, "Oh, I have lots of money. Here, I'll buy drinks for everyone if you can't afford them." Nora was a sweet young woman with a heart of gold—and a time bomb of cultural insensitivity!

It took three days for the bomb to go off. The two teen friends told her to get lost, a member of her own former church said she would "end up a loser, just like your mother," and the local mission professional was climbing the walls because of the behavior she exhibited toward the locals and toward other members of the group.

The team leader called each offending member into a private meeting individually, then addressed the issue at a team meeting. They solved the issue—actually, it was papered over—but not before realizing that the root of this problem was the failure of one person to go through team training. Nora did not know what she was getting into; the other team members had not had time to acquaint themselves with Nora's personality—and everyone suffered.

Such negative outcomes are not always the case. You can join another church group and become a positive, even vital force on the team—if you prepare properly. One of my dearest friends announced that when she came to Romania on our next short-term mission team, she was bringing her niece—who lives four hundred miles from her in Richmond, Virginia. I couldn't say no! But Donna agreed to tape or take notes of each meeting and ensure that her niece Annie would study them. A week or so later, Donna reported that a teacher friend, also from Richmond, had given her a check as the deposit to come on the mission trip. Again, how could I say no to Debbie when I had already accepted Annie?

However, what a wonderful asset to the team those two turned out to be. They gave Donna key questions to ask at team meetings. Annie and Debbie made the ten-hour round-trip drive twice to help in a team fund-raiser and for another fellowship event. By the time the trip was near, everybody had already picked Annie and Debbie to be in their various work groups. The band of individuals came together as a team from the outset, and such was the group's acceptance of the two out-of-town participants that they specifically arranged the reunion for a weekend when Annie and Debbie could drive up to New Jersey. Best of all, there were no culture shocks or embarrassing gaffes, because everybody had done their homework, whether or not they had physically attended the meetings.

So what does the team leader do today when asked to accept a mission participant who cannot join the pre-trip preparatory meetings? If the "sponsor" convinces you he or she knows the person well and that the person will fit harmoniously with the team; if the sponsor agrees to record each meeting and send the tape to the friend; and if the sponsor agrees to call the person before each meeting and bring his or her questions to be answered, then the risks are probably acceptable. This is not an area for inviolable rules. As a leader, you need to make a judgment call based partly on experience, gut feeling, and the believability of the sponsor. Accepting a person on a mission trip who gets no training, an individual who is not a team player, and one who knows nobody else present is not in anyone's interest.

WHEN PREDEPARTURE MEETINGS ARE NOT POSSIBLE

Clearly, team meetings are vital for preparing the group for the mission experience. Sometimes, though, such meetings seem logistically impossible before departure. Perhaps your team is coming from all across the country, rather than emanating from one church or community. Yet the importance in preparing them for the cultural differences, and their coming together as a team is no less. What can you do?

In such circumstances, I suggest you hold an abbreviated training session *en route* to your mission destination. It could be convened at the U.S. departure airport, if the group is meeting in a gateway city and then flying overseas together. On a trip to Prague, we had everybody booked on flights that arrived at Newark Airport around 11:00 A.M. Then we held an all-afternoon get-acquainted meeting and training session at an airport hotel before flying out together as a team that evening. If they are converging on one foreign city from numerous points, you could do it there. One team traveling to Africa flew from various U.S. and Canadian cities into Amsterdam, then planned to fly together to Nairobi. They booked rooms at an airport hotel, showered, met one another, then had a two-hour workshop. In the afternoon, the team leader broke the group into foursomes and sent them into Amsterdam on a scavenger hunt. By the time they met back at the hotel for dinner, they had already formed friendships and were coming together as one team from the disparate individuals who had tentatively introduced themselves just a few hours earlier. They had one more ninety-minute training session, then a good night's sleep before the flight to Africa.

Another option would be to have the team's training meeting after arrival at the host site. However, this is impractical for several reasons. By then the team is excited and wants to jump into their mission work. They are distracted, and some may actually not be as alert, due to the jet lag they are trying to shake. Furthermore, it could be construed as impolite to closet yourselves away from your hosts for private training meetings, which they might think should have taken place before you arrived in their midst.

You may draw your content for the meetings from the suggested agendas for the monthly team meetings that appear at the end of this chapter. Remember, however, that if you are to conduct your meetings on the day of departure, you must take everything with you. If you will be using handouts, worksheets, overhead transparencies, music tapes, a flip chart—prepare them all before you leave home. It is already a challenge to reduce eight months of meetings into a couple of hours; don't waste time by having to write things on a blackboard while the team watches.

PREPARING SPIRITUALLY FOR THE TRIP
Prayer and Scripture

The Short-Term Missions Committee of the Reformed Episcopal Church makes the following excellent suggestions for preparing yourself and your team spiritually:

> Prayer will be one of the most important ways that you can prepare for your short-term experience. Here are some suggestions of the things to pray about:
>
> Pray that you will be teachable, submissive to authority and eager to serve.
>
> Pray for your team leaders and the other members of your team.
>
> Pray that you will demonstrate love toward the people you meet.
>
> Pray for the people in the city/country where you will be serving.[1]

The committee urges each team member to memorize some verses that will encourage him as he prepares and while he serves on the project. It suggests Philippians 2:3–11. It concludes:

> Especially during the months before you leave, aim at walking consistently with the Lord. Spend quality time each day meditating on God's word. READ the book of Acts at least twice before going overseas.
>
> Continue to serve others around you and seek opportunities to share Christ with others. Practice leading a Bible study. Prepare a three minute testimony to give while overseas."[2]

Prayer should be regular and specific for your upcoming mission. Pray for the needs of your fellow team members, your hosts, and the people you will meet. Ask God to prepare your heart to be a servant, useful to the leaders and your teammates. Ask church members to pray for your spiritual development and sensitivity as you prepare for the trip.

A Time of Commissioning

Finally, here's a specific suggestion to the team leader(s) regarding the personal spiritual preparation of the team members: try to arrange for them to be commissioned by the sending church's pastor. Ideally, arrange for a commissioning ceremony during the worship service the Sunday prior to departure. It is an act that will serve to emphasize the purpose of their mission and send them out as missionaries representing the body of Christ. The commissioning should include Scripture reading, an appropriate exhortation to the group, a reminder for members to pray for the team, and a commissioning prayer led by the pastor. Other leaders, such as church elders, may join the pastor up front, placing hands upon team members before the prayer begins. The mission—its location, goals, and tasks—may be added to a program insert or briefly mentioned by the team leader.

Commissioning such *sent ones* has a direct biblical link, as we read in Acts 13:2–3 where the Holy Spirit said, "'Set apart for me Barnabas and Saul [Paul] for the work to which I have called them.' So after they had fasted and prayed, they placed their hands on them and sent them off."

PREPARING FOR EVANGELISM

Regardless of the specific tasks adopted by individual team members, they all should recognize that their participation in a Christian mission team includes some form of expressing their faith in the host community. This can appear a daunting challenge to some, and should be addressed during the training meetings. Part of each meeting for several months should be set aside for people to feel more comfortable about sharing their testimony.

Preparing Your Testimony

They may simply be asked to stand and share their faith for a couple of minutes during a visit to a worship service. In such a case, they can speak as they did when they first introduced themselves to the other team members: their name, where they are from, their vocation, marital status and descriptions of their close family, and their hobbies.

Now add a couple of positive specific observations about the host country or community: "I am struck by the awesome beauty of the mountains here in El Salvador, and have been deeply moved by the people of San Miguel who have welcomed me as if I were a member of their own family."

Next comes the easy part: Share something God has done

for you, how He has changed your life, or what makes you so grateful for what He has done for you. Pretend you are making up a thank-you note to send to God tonight. Could you think of a thing or two to say? What would you put in that note? Now jot down a couple of those thoughts and add them to the personal introduction above. *Voila!* You have a wonderful, personal testimony that the local host Christians will appreciate and enjoy.

Other members may be planning to share their testimony more widely, for example with groups, or on a door-to-door church planting campaign. Most short-termers are paired with a translator, and they could follow the model of the Global Missions Fellowship program. Here is an excerpt from GMF's *"Five Things to Accomplish with Each Visit"* training tips:

#1) Introduction of the American

The national coworkers should introduce you as an American friend and guest in their country. For example, "This is my friend John Doe, who is visiting our country from the United States. We are visiting homes in the community today. Would you allow us a few minutes during which Joe may share a special story with you? It is the story of what Jesus Christ has done with his life."

It is important to review this introduction with your national coworkers before you start your visiting. During the introduction, maintain eye contact, smile, and seek to shake hands as a friendly greeting.

#2) Testimony

Share your testimony of how you became a Christian. . . . Proceed a paragraph at a time through the testimony, alternating between English and the national language. Remember the Scripture says the word of your testimony is a spiritual weapon and can be powerfully used by the Holy Spirit. At the conclusion, ask the person you are visiting if you may ask them several questions about their relationship with God/Jesus Christ.

#3) Tract

Proceed through the GMF Evangelism Tract [or the specific evangelistic tract you're using]. Share and show verses from the Scriptures as appropriate. Pray during the presentation and particularly when the nationals are leading them in prayer.

#4) Invitation to the Evening Meeting

Provide them with all the information they need to attend the

evening meeting that has been established to welcome those having interest. Warmly encourage them to bring family and friends
as well. Ask them to be your "special guest" at the meeting.

#5) Follow-up Information

Have the national worker fill out the follow-up information
panel of the tract. This information is vital for conserving the har-
vest after the campaign.[3]

Delivering a Sermon or Message

The last type of evangelism training for the team is for members who wish to deliver a sermon or spiritual message to a
church or other assembly in your host community. Be sure to ask
your pastor or spiritual team leader for advice, and once in the
country seek ideas from the local pastor, career missionary, or
field representative. You must be aware of the differences in culture and style to which the congregations in your destination are
accustomed. A simple format that the Rev. Richard A. Carter, senior pastor at Faith Presbyterian Church in Medford, New Jersey,
teaches mission teams is as follows:

1. Pick your Scripture text.
2. Tell a personal anecdote that directly relates to the
   point of your message and the Bible verses.
3. Tell a story in simple, everyday words, that bridges the
   example from the Scripture with how that
   lesson (commandment, etc.) carries through to the life
   of people today.

Carter, who has led trips to Latin America and Eastern Europe, urges speakers to use simple language: "Avoid four-syllable
words, not only because the audience might not understand
them, but because they might confuse or stump the translator,"
he says. Indeed, even one-syllable words on occasion can do that.
Once while he was delivering a sermon on the subject of resisting
temptations, Rick maintained his natural pace as his young female interpreter did a great job of keeping up with his translation
and even his gestures as he checked off some of the deadly sins.
Then he came to "lust," and the translator stopped dead. For several seconds, the teenager stood in front of the congregation in

silence. Realizing she had heard a word she did not understand, she turned to Pastor Rick and asked, "Please explain lust." He looked at her, looked at the eagerly waiting audience, looked back at her, and said, "Never mind, skip that one!"

Rick learned an important lesson: Spend a few moments with the translator before you deliver your message. Go over your notes together, explaining your theme and point. Advise the translator of the Scripture verses you will use so he or she can bookmark the pages for quick reference. If the translator is an experienced Christian, ask whether your points seem clear or whether there might be a cultural gap as your message currently stands.

Also, avoid using humor. Unlike churches at home, congregations are not used to laughing during worship, and humor often translates poorly, especially when references to American culture are unclear. Resist making political comments, and be very careful about using hand gestures.

When selecting a sermon topic, do not choose a subject that has complex points, or which uses examples the local audience might not understand. Few people in a rural mountain village in the Andes would understand an anecdote that included an airplane. One team member's creative, well-planned sermon titled "How can you hit a home run for Jesus when you can't get to first base?" was completely lost on a Moldavian congregation who had never even heard of the game of baseball. Talking to a host community in Southern Sudan about television programming would be a total communication failure. The sermon illustration of a computer Web site would be meaningful in Alabama, but useless in Albania.

So what topics should you urge team members to cover? I believe the basics are still the best. Choose subjects that go to the heart of the faith: the story of the Cross, the Resurrection, the power of faith and prayer. Some ordained ministers spend days working on the "perfect" sermon every week. Now your team is halfway around the globe in a remote village with no on-line Internet service to do sermon research, and they ask you to deliver a sermon an hour from now. What advice can you give your team member?

"Tell me about the Resurrection and give me three examples of how it has affected your (or someone else's) life." Give that simple instruction, and your member/speaker has a sermon.

Other good areas are those that illustrate God's desire to recon-
cile mankind to Himself (such as the return of the prodigal son,
Zaccheus the tax collector, or the woman at the well). It is hard to
choose a topic more compelling, more powerful, than the basic
stories from the life of Jesus Christ. It has been said that the
Gospel is the Good News. It is an exciting story already; it needs
no gimmicks nor props; no bait to hide the hook.

A final tip for sermon planners comes from Pastor Carter.
He says that after he has prepared his weekly message, he imag-
ines himself in the audience as a member who has heard every
word and example he has just spoken. Then Carter envisions that
person asking "So what? Who cares?" Carter believes that if he
cannot answer that imagined skeptic, his message has failed.
That's a good suggestion. Such a test is as valid and imperative for
those who deliver a single message in the mission field as for the
pastor who delivers a weekly sermon to his own congregation.

Keeping the message simple and telling basic stories certainly extends to the gospel messages we give children. That is important to remember as you think of puppets, props, and fancy story
lines in ministry in another culture. One team from New Jersey
had made elaborate plans for Vacation Bible School in a different
village each day they would be in the host country. Skits were written, Bible verses rehearsed: this was a group which had taken seriously the admonition to plan ahead! The problem was, they had
not considered their audience. These were kids from ages two to
twelve who had no knowledge of the Christian message.

The children squirmed and chattered and by the time the
team was one quarter of the way into their presentation, they had
completely lost the crowd. After watching the same thing for two
or three days, one team member, Margaret Ramsey, suggested
tentatively, "Would you like me to try something tomorrow?" Other team members were frustrated by their obvious inability to
convey their message, so they readily delegated that portion of
the next day's VBS to Margaret. When the time came, she said
simply, "Would you like to hear a story?" Kids are the same every-
where, and they enthusiastically agreed.

Every day from then on, up to one hundred children sat on
the ground around Margaret as she said, "I'd like to tell you the
story about a man called Jesus . . ." For the next twenty minutes,

they were captivated by her natural, conversational style, and the simple way in which she told the story.

The first group had done a wonderful job of *preparing* for their message, but they had not considered the time it would take to tell (doubled when everything had to be translated), nor the sophistication level of their audience. Margaret offered a simply told yet powerful story and won their attention and hearts. The acronym KISS—Keep It a Simple Story—is always appropriate in the evangelism tasks of short-term overseas missionaries.

TEAM MEETING TOPICS

As mentioned earlier, you should have between eight and twelve meetings before the team departs. In this section, let's consider possible topics for ten team meetings.

The First Meeting

The main objective of the first meeting is to offer an overview of the mission trip to interested persons. Therefore the agenda is generally set as follows:

Opening prayer

Introductions of key persons (pastor, mission chairperson, team leader)

Introductions of others present

Scripture reading on the biblical basis for missions: Matthew 28:16–20 ("make disciples")

A brief (ten to twenty minutes) overview of the mission:

Where we are going

Why we are going

What we can do to help while we are there

Brief discussion of logistics:

cost, dates, fund-raising ideas, scholarship money available; expectations of team participants: financially, rules (no alcohol/tobacco), learning the language, and attendance at team meetings; journaling, health considerations, insurance, accommodations and meals, cultural sensitivity, preparation through reading Scripture and assigned materials

Questions

Adjourn with prayer

Icebreakers

To kick off your early meetings in the spirit of cross-cultural understanding, and to get to develop relationships and make new friends, here are a couple of ice-breaking exercises. The following three icebreakers will be part of the second and third meetings, which should be attended by intended trip participants. (Remember, the first meeting is primarily informational for prospective participants.)

"Me No Speak English"

Pair off each person with someone else who is not a close friend. Now ask one member of each twosome to be the designated "speaker." During the next three minutes, they are to introduce themselves to their partner, but without using the spoken word. They can gesture, draw, hum—but they may not speak or write any words or alphabetic characters. In the assigned time, they are to describe their name, work, family status, hobbies—all the things we would tell a person whom we just met and like, but without using words. After three minutes, the roles are reversed and the other partners gets the same time to describe themselves.

When the time is up, ask people to introduce their partners to the group, using only the information they gleaned from the exercise. Besides some hilarious assumptions some people will have made (Who was it who said, "The greatest problem with 'communication' is the assumption that we have achieved it"?), you can then make the serious point that learning the language of your mission trip destination is very important. Without knowing the basics, you cannot even tell a new Christian friend you just met about your own family.

Brag about a Friend

Rather than the dull, trite routine of introducing ourselves, ask each twosome to now take two or three minutes to properly introduce themselves to their partners. Provide paper and pens so that the other person can make notes. Include family details, their church, why they are going on this trip, previous mission involvement, their vocation, etc. Then switch so that their partner speaks while the first person takes notes. Asking questions is fine. When everyone is finished, the person who took the notes stands and says something like, "I'd like you to meet a special new friend of mine, and tell you why I'm glad she or he is coming with us on this team." Then the person tells the group about his or her partner. Proceed around the room until everyone is introduced. It is different; it is uplifting; and it is a start to the team-building practice that will carry on from this moment forward.

"Listen to Me"

Ask the group to form a circle inside a second circle. Then have the two rings walk around in the opposite direction. When you say "Stop!" they will pair up with the person opposite them. Now have each pair talk about a specific topic: a political controversy, describe their family, their job, the weather—you pick the subject. For one full minute they must tell their partner their opinions or details on the given topic—but both must talk simultaneously. The challenge is to listen while you are talking. After calling "Time," you should ask each person to tell their partner what they learned about him or her. Then debrief the group and ask them to share how much information was lost. The point to this exercise? It shows that when we are talking we can learn very little about the person we are with, and that the best way to learn about a person or culture is to listen.

Meetings Two Through Ten

The topics covered in the meetings that lead up to the mission trip depend on the destination, work to be done, and team's experience level. What follows are samples of the agenda from nine more monthly meetings that lead up to a typical overseas short-term mission trip where English is not the host community's language.

Second Meeting (Eight Months Before Departure)

This is the first meeting for those who have read the information, prayed, and thought about the project, and either are making (or strongly considering) a commitment to the project. As likely members of the developing team, they need to get to know each other. Therefore there are two icebreakers during this meeting (both described on the preceding two pages).

> Opening prayer
>
> Scripture reading on the biblical basis for missions: Genesis 12:1–3 (blessed to be a blessing)
>
> "Me No Speak English" exercise
>
> Introductions using "Brag about a Friend" team-building exercise
>
> Language skills: the alphabet, pronunciation, recommended phrase books, expectations of participants
>
> Financial matters: $100 deposit required by next Saturday; submit application for scholarship form now if you need help
>
> Questions
>
> Assignment of prayer partners
>
> Journal assignment: "Why am I going on this trip?"
>
> Adjourn with prayer

Third Meeting (Seven Months Before Departure)

Music is not only a powerful ministry—one that transcends many barriers—it is a wonderful component in the way we worship. It also builds camaraderie in the team. You will move a step closer to being bridge builders by learning some songs in the language of your host community. If you do not have a translator readily available, check with the music publisher, your mission host, or even the embassy of the destination country in case they can provide songs in their native language. Appendix E lists several songs that are easy to learn and often are well-known in foreign countries. Beginning with the third meeting, the team should practice several songs (recommended titles are shown).

> Opening prayer
>
> Scripture reading on the biblical basis for missions: Matthew 24:14 ("reaching all the world's people")
>
> "Listen to Me" exercise

Introductions of any new team members

Distribute list of team members with telephone numbers and any fax, and E-mail contacts

Designate team photographer, medic, spiritual leader, and music leader

Sharing the culture (team members share an item on the host country they learned recently)

Work available during the trip

Language skills: Personal introductions (Practice saying such phrases as "Hello, my name is . . .", "I am an American," "I am a Christian." See Appendix D); practice the song "Alleluia"

Financial matters: Fund-raising ideas

Recommended resources (books, Internet addresses, etc.)

Questions

Journal assignment: "How have I personally seen God at work?"

Adjourn with prayer

Fourth Meeting (Six Months Before Departure)

Opening prayer

Scripture reading on the biblical basis for missions: Luke 10:25–37 (the Great Commandment)

Introductions of new team members

Financial matters: Need to pay first financial installment by Saturday; fund-raising update

Sharing the culture (team members share an item on the host country they learned recently)

Preliminary sign-up for on-site tasks

Language skills: Practice personal introductions; count from 1 to 10; sing "Alleluia"

Questions

Journal assignment: "One experience that I definitely want to have while in the host community"

Adjourn with prayer

Fifth Meeting (Five Months Before Departure)

Opening prayer

Scripture reading on the biblical basis for missions: Luke 4:
14–19, 40–43 (Christ's mission)

Introductions of new team members

Guest speaker: Someone who has previously taken a similar
short-term mission trip

Financial matters: Fund-raising update

Sharing the culture (team members share an item on the
host country they learned recently)

Distribute preliminary worksheet of on-site task
assignments, break into small groups to discuss further
training needed, equipment/supplies required, etc.

Language skills: Say the names and relationship of your
family members; practice John 3:16; sing "Alleluia" and
learn "God Is So Good"

Logistics: Apply for passports, frequent flyer numbers, trip
cancellation insurance

Journal assignment: "The spiritual gifts I bring to this
mission"

Questions

Adjourn with prayer

Sixth Meeting (Four Months Before Departure)

Opening prayer

Scripture reading: John 13:12–20 ("We go as servants")

Introductions of new team members

Financial matters: Need second financial installment by
Sunday

Our mission as servants

Sharing the culture (team members share an item on the
host country they picked up recently)

Language skills: Learn basic questions; practice personal
introductions; sing "Alleluia" and "God Is So Good"

Journal assignment: List a Bible passage that means a lot to

you, and explain how you would present this passage in
a five-minute message while in the host community

Questions

Adjourn with prayer

Seventh Meeting (Three Months Before Departure)

Opening prayer

Scripture reading: Ephesians 1:17–19 ("Growing as
disciples")

Introductions of new team members

Sharing the culture (team members share an item on the
host country they picked up recently)

Distribute worksheet of on-site task assignments; break into
small groups to discuss further training needed,
equipment/supplies required, etc. Report from leader
of each task group

Language skills: Review progress to date; learn new Bible
verses; learn the song "I Have Decided to Follow Jesus"
and practice "Alleluia" and "God Is So Good"

Journal assignment: "How I think this trip will affect my
life"

Questions

Adjourn with prayer

Eighth Meeting (Two Months Before Departure)

Opening prayer

Scripture reading: Galatians 6:2 ("Carry each other's
burdens")

Financial matters: Need final payment by Sunday

Get copy of photo/personal details page of each member's
passport

Sharing the culture (team members share an item on the
host country they picked up recently)

Guest speaker: A national of host country to talk about the
culture, people, customs, etc.

Distribute on-site assignment worksheets. Members meet in

small groups to discuss further training needed, equipment/supplies required, etc. Report from leader of each task group

Language skills: Practice Christian phrases and pleasantries; learn specific phrases for your on-site tasks; learn "Jesus Loves Me" and practice "Alleluia," "God Is So Good," and "I Have Decided to Follow Jesus"

Journal assignment: "Something I have learned that has broadened my cultural sensitivity"

Questions

Adjourn with prayer

Ninth Meeting (One Month Before Departure)

Opening prayer

Scripture reading: Acts 1:8 (Jesus' call for geographic dispersion)

Sharing the culture (team members share an item on the host country they picked up recently)

Distribute on-site assignments worksheet. Members meet in task groups to discuss further training needed, equipment/supplies required, etc. Report from leader of each task group

Language skills: Guest speaker from host country to converse in their language; practice four songs

Journal assignment: "How I will reach out to share God's love more with a team member I have been most distant from so far"

Announce arrangements for commissioning team during worship service before departure

Questions

Adjourn with prayer

Tenth (Final) Pre-Trip Meeting (One Week Before Departure)

Opening prayer

Scripture reading: Revelation 7:9–17 (The ultimate objective)

Introductions in the host language

Trip logistics: Hand out checklist; itineraries (two copies: one to take, one to leave with family); and tickets. Offer packing tips

Financial matters: Should you bring cash, traveler's checks, or credit cards? How much spending money will you need?

Report from leader of each task group

"What if . . .?" (Preparing the team for the unexpected)

Questions

Adjourn with prayer

These agendas may not exactly fit the type of mission trip you are planning, but you can easily adapt them to your own group. Establishing the meetings firmly on Scripture and prayer reminds team members of the real reason you are embarking on the mission. You may want to set aside more time for specific training (for tasks such as a clown ministry, VBS preparations, etc.). Alternatively, subgroups, such as the construction crew or medical professionals, might prefer to hold a separate meeting to discuss their specific preparations, then report to the overall team meeting.

EFFECTIVE PLANNING

All these meetings require advance planning, of course. Begin a year in advance, thinking through the trip—then make a list. Next look carefully through that list, chronologically "thinking" yourself through the events. For example, if you have no access to a mission specialist who can provide your team with the cultural training for your host community, it is your responsibility. Preparations again! Write or call your contact in that country and pose questions such as those above. Ask for mistakes previous teams have made. Ask for previous team contacts and then ask them what they wish they had known before they left home and what advice they can offer you.

There are many things for you to check and recheck. Make a checklist just for the trip finances, with columns for each installment due and rows listing every participant's name. Then you can quickly scan to see who owes money and who has paid. Make your checklist and stick to it! You also may keep track of the amount paid as well as passport status in a passenger manifest (see Appendix B).

While leading a team to Lebanon, I asked to see each person's passport to check that no stamps from previous visits to Israel existed. Two or three times, one member forgot her passport. When I called her for the umpteenth time, she rather rudely put me in my place, telling me that she was a travel agent by profession and was insulted at being treated so childishly. When we got to Beirut Airport, I went ahead to corral the team's luggage in one place. I finally matched all the bags with my flock—except one. As a machine-gun toting militia man escorted me into an interrogation room, there was Elaine, trying to argue away her Israeli passport stamp. After sending the exhausted team on to their hotel, I returned to use all the diplomacy and reason the Lord imparted to me with the PLO officials. Finally, they waived the penalty of imprisonment, deciding instead on the lesser punishment of deporting Elaine on the 3:00 A.M. flight back to London.

The lesson? Team leaders should not take anybody's word for granted. Make another checklist for the documents you need: the liability release form, travel insurance proof, passport copy, parental permission, medical information form, and so on, and check it frequently.

Amid all these details of logistics and paperwork, do not forget a key part of your preparations: learning about the culture. Significantly, the "Sharing the Culture" exercise appears in all but three of the ten team meetings. Knowing about the region you will visit means more than just customs and history, though. In the next chapter we will continue to prepare for our missions trip by learning about culture shock, adjustment, sensitivity, and sacrifice in service.

NOTES

1. *Short Term Missions Manual*, (Warminster, Pa.: Board of Foreign Mission of the Reformed Episcopal Church, n.d.), 7.
2. Ibid.
3. *Campaign Handbook* (Dallas: Global Mission Fellowship, 1996), 7. Used by permission of Global Mission Fellowship with "attribution for the glory of our Lord and the advancement of His kingdom".

Chapter Nine

PREPARING FOR A NEW CULTURE

*H*alfway through your first mission trip to a remote village in Latin America, you are immersed in sweltering heat. For a week, you have been unaware of the outside world, cut off from newspapers and television. You've lived each day with dust in your hair, lizards in your room, and who-knows-what on your plate. And because you didn't consider it important to learn the language, you cannot even talk about your surroundings with the villagers you meet each day.

Servanthood and discipleship sounded good back home a few months ago, but now everything seems awkward, and you make mistakes. "I didn't realize men and women sit on separate sides of the church during worship. . . . How come they seemed offended when I told them I don't eat red meat? . . . But they cut off that chicken's head right in front of me. I can't eat *that!*" And early in the trip you tell your roommate, "These people smell really bad. How come they don't use deodorant?"

No one is ever fully prepared for being immersed in a new culture. It's a whole new world, so unlike American culture, where convenience and certain social customs are taken for granted. But as servants who give and want to honor the local people, we need to be able to adjust and accept these changes. With proper preparation, culture shock probably will still occur, but it will not be as jarring, and we will be more able to focus on the ministries at hand.

PREPARING FOR CULTURAL SHOCK

In an age of satellite television, travelogues, and Internet communications that make Americans more aware of the world beyond our shores, team members still can be taken aback and start to complain when things are not identical to their hometown while visiting Douala, Cameroon, or Dhaka, Bangladesh. As the team leader, be sure your members understand that this is not a luxury tour where they will be staying in hotels with room service, catered meals, and CNN by satellite. There can be dirt, humidity, unusual main dishes, and lots of different customs.

Culture shock can start when members first see the teeming masses fighting for every millimeter of sidewalk space during Hong Kong's rush hour, smell the stench of the backstreet alleys of Cairo, or spot abandoned eight-year-olds living in the sewers of Colombia. Cultural shock also occurs when we miss what we have taken for granted: no hot water for showers, the sanitary conditions of cooking facilities, the frustration of not being able to understand—nor be understood.

The very best thing a team leader can do is prepare the individuals for some sense of how this experience will be different from their home environment. When they envision the differing conditions in advance, it becomes less of a shock and a part of the adventure to which they look forward.

BEWARE OF YOUR BIASES

We can make all the preparations we want for the short-term missions trip in terms of logistics and spiritual aspects and still not be prepared when it comes to stepping into a new land, with its distinct people and culture. We must remember that the Jesus we know is the same Jesus envisioned by believers—and needed by unbelievers—in a distant land.

Sometimes, we do not really believe that truth. We may even have biases against certain peoples and races. As author and sociology professor Tony Campolo notes, "We have done something terrible. God created us in His image, but we have decided to return the favor, and we have created a God who is in our image. He comes across as a white Anglo-Saxon Protestant Republican."[1] Most of the people we will visit either will not be white or

Anglo-Saxon. They may not be Protestant nor Republican. Yet God created them all and desires all would enter His kingdom. (And many believers we will meet on our mission also will not be white nor Anglo-Saxon. Clearly, God loves them too.)

This requires cultural sensitivity and an alertness to our biases. If we are on a mission trip to Africa, we need to try to see God through African eyes. Otherwise, we will be the same cultural bulldozers our well-intentioned colonial forefathers were two centuries ago. As Christians in mission, we need to build bridges between ourselves (and our congregations) and our partners abroad. If you do not think such gaps exist, play a word association game, as I did with a team headed for Palestinian refugee camps once.

"Quickly! What's the first stereotype that comes to mind when I say the word 'Palestinian,'?" I asked. Fifteen hands went up:

"Terrorist!" many exclaimed with one voice.

"Muslim extremists!" yelled a few others.

A few months later, they were praying with people who had lived in Palestine for six hundred years and had seen their ancestral homes destroyed by U.S.-supplied bombs. They met people whose citizenship in their ancestral birthplace was stripped when the U.S. and Britain voted for the formation of the state of Israel, and now lived as stateless indigents in rat-infested hovels in a neighboring country. One more thing: These Palestinians were Christians, and had been for a dozen generations. Please do not misunderstand me. I am not making political statements nor am I opposed to the Israeli State. I am merely showing how we need to understand the culture and viewpoints of those we are visiting before we bluster into their environment and do more harm than good. By understanding both points of view, we are better equipped to build bridges of trust between people who have traditionally held each other in mistrust and animosity.

We also must be aware of cultural stereotypes we may harbor toward people in communist or former communist countries, people living in lesser developed countries, the poor, and those who are just different from us. We must remember that we are their guests and that all are loved by the God who sent His Son for their deepest spiritual needs.

LEARNING TO RESPECT CULTURAL DIVERSITY

Part of the fun and intrigue of foreign travel is the very fact that things are done differently from what we are used to. "But back home, we *always* get free refills on coffee," protested one participant as he was presented with a $15 bill for three cups of coffee in Brussels. Why was it even necessary to explain "But we're not back home; we're in Belgium" to the objector? Do not assume *anything* is "like back home," and don't complain about it when you make the discovery. Still, recognizing cultural diversity goes beyond that.

What message do you send the local Christians when halfway through your trip your team joins in the chorus of how they would kill for a Big Mac and french fries? What does that say about the food they have scrimped and saved to proudly serve you at every meal so far? In their excellent book, *Vacations with a Purpose,* Chris Eaton and Kim Hurst remind us of the Missionaries Prayer: "Where You lead me I will follow; what You feed me, I will swallow!"[2]

Recognize Differences in Cultures

Respecting cultural diversity occurs when we are able to recognize differences in the two cultures—ours and theirs. My wife once spent a summer on a student work exchange in France. Chris was upset that two of the other local girls with whom she worked seemed to ostracize her. She was fluent in French and remains a very sensitive, friendly person; yet the longer she stayed there, the less the two girls—who were the same ages—wanted to do with her. Finally, she understood. Her mother had dutifully packed her off with a suitcase filled with nice clothes, enough to have a different outfit each day. Although Chris was hardly living with poverty-stricken people, in France her peers owned two or three skirts each, and they had to wear the same clothes every two or three days. They resented Chris "flaunting" her wardrobe by having a different outfit every day.

If you are heading for a third-world construction site, and will be working alongside locals, do you think you will fit in better wearing designer jeans that obviously just came off the shelf, or older jeans with scuffs and a rip or two? Save the fashion show for a fund-raiser back home. Try to fit in with local dress customs while on a mission trip.

Teenagers often participate on mission trips. They can make many valuable contributions, and the experience is inestimable as they build life skills. But recognize that the peers with whom they fellowship in the distant country will want to talk about what it is like in America. An important part of their cultural sensitivity training is to *not* tell how they have their own private bedroom with their own telephone, computer, and color TV; or about the new car they expect to receive at graduation. We are there to build bridges with the local community. Instead, such revelations can drive a wedge between our teens and those in an impoverished community, whose loving families cannot even give them two nutritious meals each day. For that reason, it probably is not a good idea to bring *Vogue* or *McCalls* with you since these magazines reflect a way of life back home vastly different from the one they live.

Know the Cultural Rules

Research and the resultant team training can reveal many cultural rules. Knowing these customs and social rules of behavior before departing on the mission can help every team member be sensitive and more effective in their communication. Here are several cultural rules in countries far and wide:

- In Arabic countries, never refuse the obligatory coffee offered by your hosts.
- In Islamic countries, men should never inquire about the health of another man's wife or daughter.
- Travelers to the Middle East will also know to refrain from crossing their legs and showing the soles of their shoes—it is a sign of disrespect.
- In Kenya, understand that the friendly hand-wave gesture means "Come here quickly!"
- Muslim and Hindu communities consider the left hand unclean, and you should avoid touching anyone or eating with that hand—even if you are normally left-handed.
- In India and Malaysia, the head is considered the residence of a person's soul, and should never be touched—

refrain from even patting the head of a child.

- In Brazil, the hand gesture for "OK" can get you into trouble. A female friend was quite shocked at the reaction she got when asked by the waiter how she was enjoying dinner. Since he inquired at the moment her mouth was full, she gestured with the circled thumb and forefinger symbol Americans know to mean "OK," or "Perfect." However, in Brazil the gesture means "I want to sleep with you." So much for building bridges of friendship.

Rules about conversation also may be different in other cultures. Although many foreigners would consider it impolite to bring the topic up, your overseas hosts in many cultures will have probing questions about the United States. You may be asked to answer some tough questions. Questions such as:

- "Your national leaders—and even your currency—often refer to God, yet you forbid prayer in schools. Why?"
- "How can such a wealthy country have so many homeless, hungry, and poor people?"
- "How can a country lecture so much about human rights while doing business with nations where such rights are not allowed?"
- "If your nation really wants peace, why is it the world's major arms seller?"
- "Why are you preaching God's Word here, when there is an epidemic of teenage pregnancies, drug usage, and violence in your own country, and where churches go empty?"

Speak Their Language

One of the best ways to learn about a culture, as well as to develop relationships while in the country, is to learn their language. (Learning even a smattering of the language also will help you to find your way around more easily.) Most of the team meetings suggested in the previous chapter include a segment on developing language skills. I recommend learning to count to ten, knowing some phrases, being able to give part of your testimony in the language of the country you are visiting, and being able to sing a few choruses in the country's tongue. Appendix D features simple yet helpful phrases in French, Romanian, and Spanish.

Taking the time to learn some of the language displays the servant attitude you are encouraging through Bible study. It also goes a long way to show the citizens of your host community that you really do care about them and want to communicate with them.

Respect Their History and Traditions

One of the guiding principles health care professionals learn is nonmaleficence: do no harm. Many career missionaries around the world wish short-term mission groups could also be forced to take such an oath. Mission teams never intentionally cause the local mission worker such distress and embarrassment, yet some simple oversights have caused great problems.

For instance, consider the many mission work trips over the years that have entered the Transylvania region of Romania. The word *Transylvania* can barely pass through the lips of most Westerners than some crack about Dracula inevitably follows. By the time a team arrives, the only tourist site many curious members want to see is Dracula's castle—or anything to do with the man. The problem is, from an early age, Romanians are taught in school that Dracula (known to them as Vlad Tepes or Vlad the Impaler) is a national hero. Sure, a few victims may have never left his invitation to dinner, but Romanian citizens learn he was the first Romanian in centuries to rid the homeland of Turks and various other invading armies.

The Romanians of Transylvania cannot understand the morbid fascination—and do not appreciate the jokes—the guests in their country express over their national folk hero. Western missionaries have seen Romanians they considered adult Christian friends defend Dracula's actions and become clearly uncomfortable over the discussion of the dear Count. The simple solution is for short-term mission leaders to instruct their Romania-bound teams to stop the Dracula jokes and discussions at the frontier. We are in that country to build bridges, and we would think it a little weird if foreign visitors to our own country asked us to take them on sight-seeing trips to the homes of Charles Manson and John Wayne Gacey.

Respect for local beliefs may mean changing some activities or even fashion. Stefan, a California youth pastor, took a team to an East European country, where his main task was to work with local orphaned teens living in the Christian orphanage. He also planned to train the new crop of youth pastors that they had ordained, but who had received no other training. For the first five days of the trip, the team leader could not figure why the local senior pastor kept delaying Stefan's interaction with the youth ministers. Other than the odd games the team arranged directly with the local youth, there was nothing organized with them, either. For five days, Stefan waited around for the locals to come through. Finally, the local mission hosts voiced their complaint: Stefan, in a move that brought him in closer identification with the youth group kids in his home church, wore an earring. However, the local pastor had told his own youth groups that wearing any jewelry, by girls or boys, was a sin defined in Scripture. When they saw Stefan, they did as teens around the world are apt to do: they questioned their pastor's instruction. "How can you say it is a sin when he's a man—and a pastor—and he wears an earring?"

Nobody did anything "wrong" here. Stefan was not wrong. The local pastor was not wrong. Stefan forgot a basic principle when he did not remove his earring for the trip: we must be aware of the customs and beliefs of the local community and churches we will visit. In a single, innocent oversight, they had violated the "do no harm" principle and had caused embarrassment to hardworking local believers.

On another team, Rosa somehow clicked with one of the teenage orphan girls, Ellie, to such an extent that by the end of the trip she was calling her "my daughter." During the extensive predeparture meetings, it had been stressed that participants should not give money, expensive gifts, or promises of trips to the U.S. to people they met at the mission site. Rosa chose to ignore those warnings, and it was later discovered that she bestowed all of the above on Ellie. When a team leader met with her and went over her transgressions, she agreed to never repeat them; yet ten minutes after that meeting concluded, Rosa was seen giving the young girl money and more gifts. The mission hosts were furious with the team leaders.

Months later, it was learned that Rosa, after her return home, had made numerous telephone calls to the mission site, avoiding the field representative (for obvious reasons) but asking other adults whom she had met during her trip to go around town looking for Ellie. Rosa asked that they bring Ellie to the telephone in one hour, when Rosa would call back. She asked yet others to go to the American Embassy—a ten-hour road journey away—to help the teenager get a visa. When the visa was (miraculously) approved, she asked another team member to pay for the ticket because her credit card was over the limit. Worse still, she stated that she had only booked a one-way ticket because she had no intention of sending the girl back when her six-month tourist visa expired.

By ignoring cultural rules, the local missionary's guidelines, and immigration policy, one member of a mission team managed to accomplish the following:

- Create jealousy and resentment among Ellie's peers when she kept receiving clothes and other gifts from Rosa.
- Teach orphans with no material possessions that if they wanted to get a stereo, or jewelry, or U.S. dollars, they had better make friends with the next American mission team member they met.
- Alienate the mission team leaders from their local hosts.
- Cause upheaval and inconvenience to other local adults whom she made run all over town whenever she called from the United States.
- Caused Ellie to "burn her bridges" by leaving her job without giving notice, in a community where there is 40 percent unemployment among orphan youths.
- Conspired to violate U.S. immigration laws and sent a message to the girl that such blatantly unacceptable conduct was OK.

I wish I could end this anecdote by saying it is fictitious, that such events do not happen during short-term Christian mission trips. Sadly, it occurred exactly as I detailed above (though names have been changed). And I wonder, *How will Ellie come out of this? How has the kingdom of God been glorified and bridges built to our broth-*

ers and sisters in that distant land by the thoughtless actions of just one person? Perhaps Rosa meant well. She was clearly thrilled at the discovery of a girl with whom she felt a bond—perhaps the daughter for which she had always yearned. Yet in her desire to help that new special friend, a team member undercut the work of missionaries in both the sending and host communities. Sometimes, team members have to understand that they *don't* know best. They must have faith in the cultural knowledge of the host and the instructions of the team leader.

Empower for the Future

In our desire to help our host country (and ourselves) with a productive visit, we must be careful not to do too much on our own. We need to empower them for the future, not make them dependent on us. Many mission agencies have learned that lesson, training and preparing nationals to become pastors and evangelists to their own people rather than to depend on foreign missionaries.

Short-term mission teams should be aware of these concerns. Sometimes we have creative, unusual preparations for our evangelism, VBS, or other campaigns in the host community. We bring carefully built props with us; then we take them home again. Thus, the local community becomes dependent on the foreign team to continue their good work. A better idea is to use materials and supplies that are reproducible and replenishable locally, so that they empower the on-site mission partners to carry on the good work the team has taught them.

Another common mistake for some mission members is to gather occasionally in the evening for a drink. Some denominations have no prohibition against their members having a beer, and after a long day of hard manual labor in a hot country, that outing may seem appealing. But walk in the shoes of a teen from the local church whose pastor has preached on the evils of alcohol and has forbidden them to touch it. Now they see a visiting Christian mission team, whom the youth has grown to love and respect, having a beer at the local cafe after dinner. How has the credibility of the visiting mission team now been affected? More importantly, what have you done to the youth's trust and faith in the teachings of his local pastor—the professional who has to live with the consequences of your actions long after you have returned home? And will the teen who regards drinking as sin use your action as an excuse, and act in disobedience to his conscience?

You may view that scenario as unlikely; your own church group would never consider alcohol of any sort for fear of a tainted testimony. But you may do something else, ignorant of a local congregation's beliefs. Think it through. Contact the host missionary or pastor and ask about a particular activity if you are unsure of local practices. A generally sound policy is when in doubt, don't. Your witness and their walk with God are too important to claim your Christian liberty. (In the sample covenant in Appendix A, we advocate abstaining from alcohol and tobacco while participating in a mission trip.)

One church team, for instance, pondered joining our Romania project. The pastor was particularly excited as I described the opportunities to preach two or three times each day in the dozens of fledgling churches that are popping up all over the region. But she had not considered the attitudes of the culture. When I checked with Romanian leaders, they were adamant; women could not preach in the churches there. The woman pastor was so upset that she would not allow her team to go. A great opportunity was lost because of her belief that she should go and preach. The team's participation held out tremendous promise: They would have brought doctors and nurses to help at our Christian clinic and other specialists to work at the new Christian orphanage.

Losing a team of people who could have made such a difference in that needy area was sad. One choice would have been for her to lead the team anyway, ready to serve by using her spiritual gifts wherever needed. Another choice would have been for the pastor to stay behind and send on the rest of the team. Such sacrifices are part of honoring the local leaders and empowering them for the future. It also recognizes the reality that many cultures believe the Scripture calls for men alone to hold the spiritual leadership role. The recent movement toward pastoral egalitarianism among American denominations typically carries little weight outside our borders.

FINDING THE ANSWERS

To anticipate cultural conflicts, team leaders need to do proper research. Getting the answers to key questions about social customs and local practices and mission goals before you leave can prevent misunderstanding, lessen disagreements, and increase the effectiveness of your presentations. Here is a list of issues team leaders should investigate and answer long before their team departs for an overseas mission trip:

1. What does the local mission partner and community need your team to do? (Too many mission teams want to run a VBS or build a chapel, when the local community has had a dozen other mission teams run a VBS and they do not need a chapel. Yet they may need a well-baby clinic.)
2. What is the history of the Gospel in your host community?
3. What clothing should be worn by men and women during their work? Around town? To church?
4. Should women cover their heads in church? Even if just visiting an empty one? Do women and men sit on separate sides during the worship service?
5. Should women wear jewelry or makeup? (If in doubt, do not.)
6. What about wearing the cross? (This is frequently frowned upon.)
7. Do the locals stand to pray? During Bible readings?
8. What is the average income of the people you will encounter?
9. Have they been host to American mission teams previously? What were their positive/negative experiences?
10. If you are to preach there, how long do their sermons usually last? (The pastor on one team delivered a stirring twenty-five-minute sermon with a dynamic close. As he sat, the local pastor looked at the wall clock and said, "Is that it? We have forty minutes left. Can you say

something else?" To his credit, Steve stood and extemporaneously delivered another great forty-minute sermon!)

11. Do the host congregations at your destination speak in tongues, privately or publicly? Be sure you can respect their position; otherwise it is best not to participate with the church.

12. What is the local missionary/host pastor's view on alcohol and smoking? (We ask each team member to refrain from using either tobacco or alcohol while in the host community, regardless of the local attitude.)

13. What is the local attitude toward women? This is an especially sensitive issue in Muslim areas.

14. If you have women on your team who expect to speak in churches (either to preach, teach, or give a testimony), find out whether this is permissible.

15. Would the host pastor approve your issuing altar calls in your sermon?

16. May you serve Communion to church members? The youth group?

17. Should you be prepared to give small gifts to people you meet and work with? Are there any taboos about which you need to be aware?

18. Is there any restriction on taking the supplies to fulfill your mission (medical supplies, Bible tracts, tools, etc.) into your host country, or through intermediate countries through which you must transit by surface?

You can learn a lot about the culture of your host country by checking with mission agencies that serve the area. Also ask field representatives of your (or another) denomination, the cultural attaché of that country's embassy or consulate in your nation's capital, and even inquire over the Internet.

I encourage team members to watch the newspapers, magazines, bookstores, and electronic media for items of interest on political, cultural, or religious news from the host country. During the team meetings, a few minutes are set aside for them to share the news in the "Sharing the Culture" segment. You will discover that people who had been oblivious to a certain country suddenly find a constant stream of cultural information once they make it their focus. This exercise helps close that gap between us and our partners.

When you do communicate by mail with the field, allow much longer than domestic mail delivery. Airmail letters may take four weeks to reach developing countries—even longer to arrive in remote regions of Africa and Asia. If you are corresponding by fax, many developing countries require a central fax at the post office, so be aware that others may read what you write.

Much has been said of eliciting information about your host community, but remember to also express your team's expectations to your host, in advance. If you are planning to build something, the mission host might need permits that require lengthy applications. Ask whether they will need money before your arrival to ensure that materials and supplies are waiting for your team. Tell the field representative that you are coming with the servant attitude of doing what they need, not what *you* want to do, and ask for an honest response from the outset for everyone's benefit. He or she will be overjoyed by your approach, and you both will avoid those awful, "But I thought we were going to . . ." comments at the end of the trip.

NOTES

1. Tony Campolo, "Challenging the Church with Missions," in Michael J. Anthony, ed., *The Short-term Missions Boom* (Grand Rapids: Baker, 1994), 20.
2. Chris Eaton and Kim Hurst, *Vacations with a Purpose* (Elgin, Ill.: David Cook, 1993), 94.

Chapter Ten
※
THE DAY OF DEPARTURE

$\mathscr{T}$he final team meeting should take place about one week before departure. With the day of departure in sight, this could be the most exciting gathering you have held, with a sense of anticipation, fun and team spirit such as you have not seen in previous meetings. Unlike those earlier get-togethers, this one has a single focus: the trip logistics and last-minute needs for the mission tasks.

At this final meeting the team leader might give team members copies of their own individual sheet that they completed after the first meeting, on which they wrote down their reasons for participation, their personal goals for the trip, and their concerns. "How do you feel now?" you should ask. "Do you feel less concerned today? What can you (and the team) do to help you attain your goals?" Supporting each other not only helps the individual and strengthens the team, it is a step along our path toward servanthood.

On the Sunday before departure, try to have each team member attend the same worship service and be commissioned as missionaries of the sending church. The sixth chapter of Acts describes how the apostles laid hands on the chosen disciples before sending them into the world to build the kingdom of God. It is no less important today that our pastors, elders, deacons, and congregations see their "sent ones" as they prepare to depart, and commit to pray for their work and wisdom. Suggestions on the content of a commissioning ceremony appear in chapter 8 (page

145

115). This can be a moving occasion, one that brings together all the months of meetings and planning and helps focus the participants' attention on the spiritual reasons for their trip.

At the preceding meeting (the ninth meeting using the recommended schedule in chapter 8), each person should provide day and evening telephone numbers and the name of their home contact while they are on the trip. Put those names into a "telephone tree," and at this final (tenth) meeting give two copies to each member. For some reason, despite the cost of international telephone calls, many travelers feel the deep need to call across the world, awakening their families in the middle of the night to say, "We've arrived!" The telephone tree will avoid twenty people having to do that.

Give each traveler two copies of the trip itinerary. Forget the one your travel agent staples to the tickets. You want all important information on one page: airline flights, meals served, bus trip times, hotel names with telephone and fax numbers (including the entire telephone dialing sequence from home), when to make time zone adjustments—even the "Dial USA" access numbers for AT&T, MCI, and Sprint from each country through which the team transits. (A sample itinerary appears as Appendix C.)

Revisit any important rules such as the ban on drinking alcohol or using tobacco. If the leader asks for "Rule number one?" and after almost a year of training, the team shouts back, "Be flexible!" the training has worked.

TIPS FOR TRAVEL

During the final predeparture meeting, go through everything people want to know about, in chronological order: tips on packing, the luggage allowance, when and where to meet, spending money, the trip itself, and team behavior. As the team leader, share any tips you have learned from experience. Here are several that I have found to be helpful:

- Take resealable plastic bags for each currency you will be handling. (Nothing is more frustrating than trying to pay for an item with a handful of coins in four currencies.)
- Take lots of one-dollar bills. Even if you have not convert-

ed money, dollar bills are acceptable and welcomed as tips in most countries.

- Take a money belt or shoulder harness to keep cash, passports, etc.
- Keep traveler's check numbers apart from the checks, and make an extra copy of the numbers that a friend can carry.
- If someone is on a special diet, the person can call the airline's toll-free reservations number and order a special meal. These range from meals for children, low-calorie meals, seafood, vegetarian, low-sodium, nonlactose and a dozen other types. There is no additional charge, but one should call at least forty-eight hours before the flight and again the day before to reconfirm that the airline has the request in their computer.
- Take a spare pair of glasses with you. It will be virtually impossible to replace lost or broken glasses in most developing countries. Even if it is an old pair, or an inexpensive pair of drugstore magnifiers, consider the alternative, and plan in advance.
- Take a list of names and addresses of friends and sponsors with you. It will be less bulky than an entire address book. Some well-organized folks print a sheet of address labels from their computer before they leave home. During your mission, send notes from the field to your supporters, telling them how helpful their financial and prayer commitment has been. Give a brief report of an exciting incident from your day. Your letter will be encouraging, and will also sow the seed for their future support of missions.

Concerning this final tip, you can prepare a simple, one-page record of those to whom you should write from the field. It would look like the grid on the next page and contain lines for all your supporters, whether five or twenty-five.

NAME	ADDRESS	SENT/NOTES

PACKING THOSE BAGS

With the day of departure so close, you may want to elaborate on some of these points (or provide some handouts listing these). Here are specific recommendations on packing and bringing spending money.

Packing Tips

Remember that nobody should pack a passport, money, or needed medications. Indeed, don't pack anything valuable in your checked baggage. Not only are there active theft rings where baggage handlers can open any locked suitcase in seconds, the airlines' limit of liability is incredibly low and filled with exclusions. The greater risk is that your bag will be misrouted. Arriving at Moscow's immigration desk will not gain you access to Russia if your passport is in your suitcase, now sitting at Milan's baggage claim following your change of planes. Neither will your blood pressure be calmed if you realize your medication is in the same bag.

Think it through: "If I am separated from my suitcase for three days, what *must* I have with me?" You can wear the same jeans and shoes again, you can wash out socks at night, but maybe you should pack the camera, toothbrush, and pill box in your carry-on bag.

Here are twenty packing tips for a more pleasant trip:

1. Always carry prescription medications in their original pharmacy-supplied bottle. If you are taking a narcotic, carry a letter of explanation from your doctor, also. Taking a copy of the prescription (with the generic, rather

than a brand name) can also help you in replacing or refilling the medication while away.

2. If you are taking your own toilet paper, drive your car slowly over the roll. It will flatten it and require much less packing space.

3. Pack a small sewing kit with a few safety pins. They can be lifesavers!

4. If you carry detergent in your suitcase, buy a small packet and bring it in that original container. Should foreign customs open your bag to find white powder in a Baggie, you may find your newfound language skills somewhat taxed!

5. A travel clothesline takes little room and can be a great help in drying clothes. If you really need clothes hangers, bring your own.

6. Take a small battery-powered travel alarm clock.

7. Avoid taking wrapped gifts. The airline security people have the right to open them. Do not pack anything in your suitcase that has the batteries installed.

8. Don't take anything you do not need. Leave the valuables at home. Instead of the bulky camera with the separate flash gun and three lenses, why not take a simple compact camera? Go through your wallet and purse and purge them of credit cards and items you will not need during your trip.

9. Couples traveling together should each pack one change of clothes in each other's suitcase, in case one bag goes astray.

10. Leave the economy sizes of soap and shampoo at home. Instead, take the leftover travel sizes you have used in hotel bathrooms. (After all, the maids will simply throw away the opened containers.) Or ask a frequent-traveler friend to save some for you. If you do not have access to those, buy the trial size toiletries from a discount drugstore. Never fill the bottles completely. Instead, leave space at the top of the bottle, then squeeze the air out as you affix the cap. This will result in a vacuum that serves to seal the bottle. Always pack liquids in a seal-

able plastic bag before placing them in your toiletries kit.

11. Bring snack food that is durable to pack. One of the highlights of the team's day will be to return to base after a hard day's work and fellowship together during a "happy hour" of granola bars or your favorite snack food.

12. A small foldable umbrella or lightweight windbreaker with a rain hood is great to have along in case of inclement weather.

13. Avoid patterned outfits in favor of neutral solid colors that you can mix and match. Fabrics such as wool, synthetics, and knits tend not to wrinkle.

14. If the voltage and/or the electric plug shape in your destination is different, take a voltage converter and plug adapter with you. Be careful: they often sell these separately. Your new 220 volt converter will not do you any good when you discover your plugs won't fit into the socket. You can pick up these converter/adapter kits at most hardware stores, and the big office supply superstores discount them.

15. Place your heaviest items on the bottom of your suitcase, separating the layers with tissue paper or plastic dry-cleaning bags. Fill the edges of your case with socks, handkerchiefs, etc., and stuff that dead space inside shoes with the same accessories.

16. Wear your bulkiest clothes and never take up valuable suitcase space with overcoats, umbrellas, pocketbooks, or cameras. You may carry them on board beyond the airline's stated baggage limits, then store them in the overhead compartment. (Always turn suit jackets or sports coats inside out before folding and placing them in the overhead bin, and always look in the bin before deplaning to ensure your wallet or passport has not slipped out.)

17. If your suitcase is hard to close, drop it onto the floor (onto the wide side). This will cause everything to settle, making closure possible.

18. If you collect physicians' samples of medications to take on your mission trip, you can save perhaps 90 percent of the packing space by discarding the promotional literature and bottles inside boxes within boxes. Combine dozens of the same pills into one larger pill bottle. Clearly mark the bottle with the drug name and strength, never mix different drugs or dosages in the same bottle, and attach a couple of copies of the package inserts to the bottle.

19. If you are taking clothes, tools, or supplies that you plan to leave at the mission site, use a foldable bag which you can then bring home inside your other suitcase. Not only is it inconvenient to have another bag to carry home (and wait for in baggage claim), a checked empty bag arouses suspicion. I have had team members pulled from the airplane boarding line by security police who interrogated them as to why they checked an empty suitcase.

20. Take a large ball of brightly colored wool to the last team meeting. I am talking bright, like Day-Glo shocking pink! Ask each team member to firmly tie a piece of this to the handle of each piece of checked luggage. When you arrive at your destination, you will immediately identify at the baggage claim carousel your Samsonite from the thirty other identical suitcases, and make assembling the team's bags much easier.

Packing Equipment for Your Mission

Pardon the cliché, but do not put all your eggs in one basket! With mission teams, what would you do if you arrived at your destination in Honduras and discovered the suitcase with *all* your week's VBS supplies was missing? Evangelism is tough without those bilingual tracts and Bibles, too. Distribute such supplies among the luggage of several team members so that you are not faced with a disaster if a single bag is lost.

For trips into "closed" countries, where evangelistic media are forbidden, you need to talk with mission experts who are experienced in that specific country to learn how you will import your supplies. Do not take this subject lightly. Border guards in such countries as Afghanistan, Saudi Arabia, Iran, and China will not smilingly accept attempts to smuggle dangerous propaganda (in their eyes) as an innocent oversight.

If you are planning to send anything that contains chemicals, gases, solvents, paints, or such contents that are not normally flown on a passenger aircraft, check well in advance with the airline's cargo department. They all have toll-free telephone numbers. Do not entrust this investigation to your travel agent, consolidator, or airline passenger staff.

A medical mission team to East Europe had previously shipped over a donated X-ray machine. Realizing that there would be no X-ray solvents and developers in that impoverished region, one of the radiologists donated $2,000 worth of the vital supplies. Since the team leader was leaving two days before the group and U.S. Airways had approved the free shipment of these thirteen cartons to accompany him on his flight to Frankfurt, it made sense for him to take the solvent. Ten minutes before boarding, the airline paged him at the gate.

"What the devil do you think you're doing?" an obviously rattled person yelled at him through the telephone. "What is in these cartons?" The group leader calmly answered his questions with the reassurance that they simply contained harmless X-ray developer. "Harmless!" the man yelled, his pitch even higher, "The cartons from the factory have a skull and crossbones on them. These are considered hazardous materials. They're coming off the airplane—and you just caused a delayed flight."

Passengers began boarding the aircraft as the team leader hung up. He asked to speak to a supervisor. Then her boss. Next they got the captain. Then he called the head of public relations at the airline's headquarters (after all, the flight was now delayed!) They did not budge a single inch. He left for Frankfurt fifty minutes later with no X-ray supplies.

Here is the postscript to the story. The rest of the team was following two days later on British Airways. One of them took the cartons and checked them in on his flight. "What is in the thirteen boxes, sir?" asked the British Airways agent. "X-ray developer and solvent," he responded. "Fine. Here is your boarding pass showing all your bag claim tags. Welcome aboard!" she said. They never blinked an eye at the cartons—skulls, crossbones, and all.

U.S. Airways was not wrong in this story. The air carrier had carefully drawn safety rules that numerous knowledgeable experts approved and that became its policy—accepted by the country's highest aviation regulatory authorities. The airline could not —and should not—compromise what it considers to be safety precepts for me, for you, for any mission team. Maybe British Airways has different regulations. Yet if they had not been blessed with that miracle, the mission team would have had two members on-site for a week with no way of demonstrating the equipment they had spent so much trouble and money getting to the host community.

The lesson for the future is that when team leaders discover the probable presence of unusual materials in the luggage, they should check to ensure the airline will accept it. If not, you can use that knowledge to investigate such alternatives as air cargo shipments (less restrictive than passenger planes, but very expensive), or ocean freight.

Luggage Allowance

Trip planners should clearly define the airline's baggage limits. They all vary, so they cannot be quoted here. Be careful to ascertain whether there are size *and* weight limits. A policy might be: two checked bags. One not to exceed 70 dimensional inches, the other no more than 55 dimensional inches and neither bag to weigh more than sixty pounds.

To arrive at "dimensional inches," add the length, height, and width together. Seventy inches sounds huge, until you add up the considerable length and girth of an expandable duffel bag. What about that bag filled with donated Bibles, medical journals, or construction tools? If it weighs seventy pounds, it is over the limit, no matter the size. The result is that you are liable for excess baggage charges on the entire bag, not just on the ten extra pounds. A seventy-pound suitcase from Chicago to Moscow costs $110, according to Air France.

These are "worst case" conditions. In reality, most carriers will let a bag slip through, even if it is a little larger or heavier than the limits. But remember that it's the check-in agent's judgment call, and several airlines have established employee incentive programs where the passenger is the loser. An airline may tell its employees: "June is excess baggage month. For every dollar you can collect in excess baggage fees, you will earn a bonus." It is a legitimate, published charge, and such collections help the company's profitability. So be forewarned!

If you know in advance that your team will have extra bags, try these tips:

1. Negotiate in advance with your group contact for them to enter a note in your computer record authorizing a certain number of extra bags.
2. "Pool" your bags by checking in as a group. If three members each had one extra suitcase, the vigilant check-in agent might charge for them. However, if you have three extra bags among 20 people, it seems less significant.
3. Ask for a supervisor and request (do not "demand") his or her intervention after explaining that you are missionaries carrying humanitarian relief supplies (or whatever they are). When they learn that you are not business executives on expense accounts, you will rarely encounter an airline supervisor who will charge your mission teams for excess baggage.

Most airline employees are decent, reasonable people, trying to balance the fiscal obligation to their employer with their other duty of delivering good service to the passenger. They get yelled at and treated rudely day after day, often for circumstances that are beyond their control. If you talk to them abruptly, they have the ultimate response: "I am just following the rules. You pay, or the bag stays." When you step into their shoes and treat them with courtesy, an understanding for their position, and humbly explain your mission and request, you will find that they respond in your favor virtually every time.

SPENDING MONEY

Team leaders should find out in advance the answers to these frequently asked questions:

"How much money should we take with us?"

"What can we buy when we are there?" (You will need to advise them whether they can buy film, batteries, sanitary supplies, and what kind of souvenirs to look for.)

"Can we use credit cards or traveler's checks at our destination?"

"How easy is it to change money? If I take traveler's checks, should I take them denominated in U.S. dollars or another currency?"

In your communication with your field representative, ask him or her to give you a complete briefing on the topic of money. When I brief mission teams that I am helping, I even advise them to avoid $100 bills (often rejected overseas because there are so many forgeries), and to refuse any banknotes with handwriting on them. (Refer to chapter 5 for more information about using credit cards, cash, and ATM cards abroad.)

Team members will want to know what they may and may not bring home through customs. Other than the obvious "no narcotics, no fruits and plants," the team leader should *not* prepare a listing of what they permit. You cannot be expected to keep up-to-date on these rules and you should not place yourself in a position of liability when a traveler says, "But he told me. . . ." I suggest that team leaders give every member the brochure "Know Before You Go" available free from the U.S. Customs Service at (202) 927-6724.

SHEPHERDING YOUR FLOCK EN ROUTE

The day of departure is here. Assuming you are traveling overseas by jet, keep in mind that the experience and knowledge of air travel among team members will vary widely. Prepare them properly for the flight.

"David, I *must* talk to you. I have some important questions that have been bothering me." Such was the urgent plea from a teenager about to make his first airplane flight. As I ushered him in and asked what was on his mind, the young man said, "That flight from Chicago to Vienna and on to Sarajevo is going to take thirteen hours. Is there a kitchen aboard where I can cook something for dinner, or will the airline check my pockets to see if I sneak a sandwich on with me?"

When I explained that Austrian Airlines would feed him— absolutely free—he was amazed. Then another thought came to him. "What about drinks?" he asked, thinking about his small travel allowance. "They probably charge a fortune to that captive audience. Will they fine me if I carry on my own fruit juice?"

Again, I explained that he could order soft drinks, water, juice, as often as he wanted, and that it would be free. I still remember the incredulous look on his face as those accumulated fears suddenly disappeared.

The frequent traveler may have read the preceding anecdote with disbelief. But team leaders should never overestimate the knowledge of their participants, especially on an overseas trip. Some will be making their first flight; others still are nervous about air travel after several flights. Our duty as team leaders is to hold their hands; to walk them through the experience in advance; to show them what to expect; and to illustrate that they are in good hands.

Starting at the airport, I suggest team leaders give participants the check-in times and tell them where to go. Despite the prospect of spending many hours traveling, you should still urge people to arrive at the airport two hours before the departure time. Lines will be shorter, staff will be less harried, and if there is a problem such as a flight cancellation, you will be the first in line to get the scarce seats on another airline.

I strongly urge team leaders to have the group check in together. While one person is counting all the bags to ensure the numbers of bags and bodies all arrived, go to a check-in supervisor and tell them you have X number of passengers and Y number of bags. At the ticket counter, suggest that it would make your group and the other passengers much happier if the airline could assign a specific agent for the group. Then have all the passports, tickets, and bags taken to that agent. Remember the total number of checked bags and review each claim check to ensure the number and destination airport are correct. When the airline agent returns the tickets, have each passenger check that they pulled only the relevant flight coupons. Three people on each of two recent mission teams had an extra flight coupon accidentally pulled. When they checked in for the return flight, there was no flight coupon. (They did get the tickets reissued, but only after an annoying ninety-minute wait and a mad dash to the gate.)

All passengers should be warned about such seemingly obvious topics as humor. Don't even think about making wisecracks referring to Cuba, hijacking, or weapons—in fact purge those very words from your vocabulary when near an airport or airline. Once, having just been bumped from a flight, I then was rewarded with a seat when one of the "lucky" passengers made a joke to the flight attendant about their arrival time in Havana. The distinctly unsmiling faces of the police and FBI agents as they hustled off the handcuffed passenger that night in Pittsburgh will be with me forever.

During the final team meeting, team leaders should have described the flight; its duration; the meals to be served (or not served!); whether a movie would be offered, and whether a charge exists for the entertainment system. At the final meeting, be sure to tell members when and how much to adjust their watches for time zone changes. If there is a connection en route, ask everybody to wait outside the aircraft jetway upon arrival until the entire team is together, then make the transfer as a group. (You cannot have twenty-five people wandering all over an international airport with the team leader hoping they will make the connection.)

Upon arrival at the destination airport, the group will be separated as you go through immigration (passport control). Leaders should remember to clearly brief team members if you are going to a "closed" country on what they should state as the purpose of their visit. If they are to avoid stating "church planting and evangelism" to the immigration officer, make sure each team member knows that at the final team meeting, not when you visit them in the airport interrogation room.

If you pooled the group's bags, remind individuals not to go through customs when they find their own suitcase. Ask the team members who arrive at baggage claim first to start hauling off all the team bags into one spot. (Now you see the logic of that brightly colored yarn!) When all the members are in baggage claim and all the bags are in, go through customs together.

Remember to give people time to change money, purchase refreshments for the bus ride ahead, and always make each team member responsible for seeing that his own bags get loaded onto and off the bus.

Try to think ahead, so if you can delegate one person to wait until the last team member gets through immigration, you can go ahead and find the bus driver and instruct the team where to go next. That sort of planning and execution really puts your group at ease.

Perhaps you have a long bus ride. If so, here are other ways you can plan ahead. Find out if the vehicle will have air conditioning and a rest room. If one or both are missing, advise the team in advance about what they should expect and plan more frequent breaks. Similarly, learn whether the bus has a cassette player. If it does, why not invite team members to bring their favorite selections of tapes—perhaps someone could be the rolling disc jockey, whiling away the miles to the sound of popular songs, the music you plan to present onsite, and some language practice sessions.

IN-FLIGHT COMFORT

You board the jetliner for a trip of several thousand miles, spanning seven to seventeen hours, depending on your destination. Even in the jumbo aircraft that ply the skies, that's a long time in a confined space, with gradual pressure changes as well. Here are some ways you can improve your comfort level during the flight.

If you are prone to earache during ascent and descent of an airplane, try these tips: (1) keeping your lips closed, gently blow to relieve the pressure in your eustachian tubes; (2) try swallowing several times; (3) chew gum or suck on a lozenge or hard candy during takeoff and landing. If you have a cold, or if the above methods do not work, use a nasal spray or take a decongestant an hour before takeoff and an hour before landing.

If you are prone to motion sickness, you should take products such as Dramamine one hour before takeoff. A follow-up dose may be required for long flights, so be careful not to pack the bottle in your suitcase. Unique bands that put acupressure on the wrists are effective in eliminating motion sickness for many people and can be used repeatedly. If you cannot find them locally, give Magellan's mail order a call at 800-962-4943.

Airplanes are hollow tubes filled with people of disparate origin, many of whom are afflicted with coughs, colds, and worse. The germs they exhale are recirculated and inhaled by the other passengers repeatedly for hours on end. Taking large doses of Vitamin C for three days before and after a flight can help build your immunity to the common ailments of others. That pillow you were about to place next to your face to sleep for the next nine hours has probably not been changed for at least twenty-four hours. Many airlines do not change pillows after every flight, and some do not even bother replenishing them daily. Why risk using the pillow a previous passenger has wheezed and sneezed into all the way across the ocean? Many experienced travelers buy their own inflatable neck pillow, considering them to be more comfortable anyway.

A jetliner's cabin air is drier than that over a desert. To help your general feeling of well-being, use a moisturizer and saline eye drops several times during the flight. Using a tiny atomizer of fresh water every hour or so not only feels good, it relieves the tension of the flight. Drinking a glass of water or juice once each hour can restore moisture to your body and reduce travel fatigue. Flight attendants often circulate with water and other beverages several times during a flight; accept each offer.

Remove your shoes and elevate your legs if possible. Since few coach seats have rising leg supports, make a point to walk around the cabin once an hour or so to improve your circulation. Wear loose or tieable shoes or you could discover that they will not fit when you go to put them on after landing. If that happens, do not worry. Your feet and ankles will return to their normal size in about ten minutes.

DEALING WITH JET LAG

Even experienced travelers should be informed about jet lag. If you are embarking on a north-south journey, there will be none! Jet lag is a physiological phenomenon that only affects passengers who traverse time zones from east to west and vice versa. The more zones you cross, the worse it can be. Here are some tips:

• Start the journey well-rested. If heading east, an extra couple of hours sleep for two or three days before your trip will be a good investment.

- When flying west, go to bed later than normal for a day or two before you travel.
- Set your watch ahead to the current time at your destination. The fact that you start thinking it is that time helps your mind and body to adjust.
- Avoid drinking alcohol and caffeine during the flight.
- On night flights, try to sleep as much as possible. On flights that arrive late at night, try to stay awake so that you will be tired and then sleep when you arrive, during their nighttime.
- When you arrive, try to conform with the local times as much as possible. If you take a mid-afternoon nap upon arrival, it will feel great, but you are just delaying your body's adjustment, and will then have trouble sleeping during the local nighttime.
- For the first couple of days after traveling, eat lots of proteins for breakfast and lunch, carbohydrates for dinner.
- Write for the U.S. Department of Energy's free "Anti-Jet Lag Diet." It requires following a rather strict regimen for a few days before your flight, but it works! It is available free for a stamped, addressed envelope from: Argonne National Laboratory, 9700 So. Cass Avenue, Argonne, IL 60439 (telephone: 630-759-8901).

One final point. Recent press attention has focused on the hormone melatonin as a magic jet lag antidote. The respected British medical journal *Lancet* reportedly claimed that melatonin reduced the effects of jet lag by as much as 50 percent. U.S. officials seem less enthusiastic: the Federal Aviation Administration does not recommend melatonin for use by pilots, and the U.S. Air Force forbids its use by their own flight crews.

When you finally touch down at your final destination, you may be a little tired. A relatively quiet first day can rejuvenate your team (see next chapter), but the anticipation will also sustain many on the team. And now, let the short-term mission begin!

Chapter Eleven

※

FINALLY THERE

*Y*ou've arrived! After a year or more of planning, you and the team are finally there. But the logistics and issues are not over. This chapter will help you in preventing the unnecessary and in troubleshooting the unavoidable. From good health in a new setting to finding lost passports and dealing with personality conflicts and the mission itself, here are many ways to make your mission project more effective in Christ's service.

FOR YOUR HEALTH

You already know to take all the medications you need with you, but do not overlook the nonprescription remedies, too. The well-stocked shelves of multiple-choice brands common in our hometown drugstores are unheard of in developing countries. Not only are familiar brands difficult to find, some over-the-counter medicines sold overseas are considered dangerous by U.S. medical authorities and cannot be sold in the United States for their alleged side effects. So bring the Pepto-Bismol, the pain relievers, the sunscreen, and the insect repellent with you.

Watch the Diet

When living in a foreign country, realize that pasteurization, refrigeration, and sanitary practices are suspect. Avoid rare (and raw) meat and fish, street vendor food, unpasteurized milk or derivatives, raw leafy vegetables, and foods made with cream, mayonnaise, and the like. Do not overeat. Experts say that our bodies only require two-thirds of our normal caloric intake while in hot climates, and the more food we eat, the greater the risk of ingesting something that disagrees with the digestive system.

You must find out in advance how safe the water is to drink. That crystal-clear babbling brook probably contains millions of parasites and should be reserved for swimming and photo opportunities. To be on the safe side, it is a good idea in any developing region to buy bottled water (check for a sealed cap). Unless you have been categorically assured of the safety of the water at your base camp, use the bottled water to brush your teeth and to mix with the drink mix you may have brought with you. Avoid ice cubes, fresh salads (where they probably washed the lettuce in tap water), and any fresh fruit you did not peel yourself. A variety of excellent, effective water purification systems (good for one person or a group) are available by mail order or from camping supply stores.

Hailed as "the widest selection of travel accessories currently available from a single source," by the *Washington Post*, Magellan's, a mail-order company, has everything from packable ponchos to hotel-room intrusion alarms and airplane evacuation smoke hoods. The company will send you a catalog packed with all kinds of useful products for travelers if you call them at 800-962-4943. (They offer a discount to groups.)

Using bottled carbonated water may be a safe way to go, but if you have ever tried brushing your teeth with it, you will see a foaming rabid-looking creature staring back at you through the mirror. Hardly the taste to start the day. On the Go Products of Albuquerque, New Mexico, manufactures toothbrushes that come filled with a special toothpaste that requires no water. This and their companion pocket shaver are great products for travel into remote areas and can be found in some supermarkets and drug store chains. You can call On the Go (505-343-9950) for a distributor near you.

Watch The Sun

If your team will be working outside, avoiding the sun when it is most ferocious is best. In equatorial areas, near water, or at high altitudes, that can be from around noon until 3:00 P.M. It is not because of laziness that the locals in those areas take siestas during the midday heat wave. Thus, if you are leading a construction team in a hot climate, try to work from early morning—say, 6:30 A.M. to 11:30 A.M.—then do not return to the job site until 3:00 in the afternoon.

Remember to warn your people who will be working outside in the sun to drink lots of water, to take an extra pair of sunglasses, a wide-brimmed hat, and plenty of sunblock, insect repellent, and light-colored clothing. Several sun lotions now include insect repellent. Such dual-purpose products are best. Each worker should take a water bottle, or take their own purified water from the base camp to the work site each day.

Be Ready for Medical Emergencies

A wise team leader will have appointed a medic during the preparations for the mission trip. It is a good idea to take a basic first-aid kit. Don't buy one of those bulky, expensive boxes. Just assemble your own and keep items in a large, sealable plastic bag. Include at least the following ingredients:

Band-Aids	Antidiarrheal medicine
Ace bandages	Antibacterial ointments
Heat/cold packs	(for cuts, etc.)
Analgesics	Laxatives
Decongestants	Antihistamines
Fever reducers	Sunburn relief
Pepto-Bismol	

Before you leave home, check with the Centers for Disease Control and the State Department's Travel Advisory Service (202-647-5225) for health warnings in your destination, and learn how to spot the symptoms and treat those ailments.

Whether or not the team has a team medic, the team leaders should consider becoming certified in cardiopulmonary resuscitation (CPR) and the Heimlich maneuver before leaving the United States. Both procedures are virtually unknown in the developing world and can be learned in about three hours. One of my most daunting memories is of the night a friend keeled over from a heart attack while eating dinner at my table during a Rotary Club meeting. There were fifty-five members—intelligent business owners and leaders all—in that club, and not one of us knew how to save Bill's life. How would you feel if that happened to a member of your mission team? Call, or have your designated team medic call, your local hospital, first-aid squad, or American Heart Association chapter for dates and details.

For serious medical emergencies, having a list of doctors you can trust is a major plus. An excellent resource is the International Association of Medical Assistance to Travelers (IAMAT). They maintain a directory of English-speaking certified doctors in more than 500 countries and geographic regions and for a donation will send you that list prior to departure. You also will receive a membership card that entitles the bearer to preestablished charges for medical attention. (You can reach IAMAT at 417 Center Street, Lewiston, NY 14092 (telephone: 716-754-4883; fax is 519-836-0102).

Another key source for information on doctors while on the mission itself is the local missionary contact. He or she probably can answer such questions as: Do hospitals screen blood supplies there? What is the doctors' level of expertise? How will they want to be paid?

Don't forget to carry your sealed envelope with the medical information forms completed by team members back at the group's formation. Your ability to advise a doctor of the patient's blood type and medical history could help save the person's life. Should a team member require a blood transfusion during the trip, medical experts suggest the following priority of donors: (1) an adult member of the mission team; (2) an adult career missionary; (3) a youth member of the mission team; and (4) a blood bank onsite from which blood testing can be verified.

All team members should avail themselves of travel insurance that covers them for medical evacuation if they are headed to less-developed countries. If you have a team going to do inner-city work in Germany, for example, there is no need to worry about evacuations; modern facilities are adequate in such urban centers. Indeed, a member's current medical insurance may have a rider that covers medical emergencies overseas.

However, think it through in advance: You are headed for Albania, where there is no screening of hospital blood supplies for viruses such as HIV or hepatitis. Even if the team member's insurance may pay for the member's hospital stay, you do not treat her in a hospital there. It is unreasonable to expect the insurer to fly Aunt Sue back to Ohio in a Lear jet, but you at least want them to fly her to a modern hospital in Rome or Vienna (via a medical evacuation, or medevac) where her treatment and chances of survival are infinitely better. When she is well enough to return home, the policy should also provide for any difference in airfare, also. A list of foreign travel insurance providers is provided in Appendix F. Read the policies carefully and pay special attention to the coverage limits, what it takes to qualify for medevac, and preexisting conditions.

The U.S. Embassy or Consulate abroad will refer you to English-speaking doctors, but cannot help you pay the bill, nor will they fly you home.

DEALING WITH THE UNEXPECTED

In a different country, literally thousands of miles from home, you can expect the unexpected. Some of the developments are minor; others, however, can bring havoc to a member or much of the team. Here are some suggestions on how to deal with the unexpected, which can begin as soon as the team arrives and goes to pick up their luggage.

Lost or Misrouted Bags

You can help avoid lost or misrouted bags by taking two steps: (1) ensure the traveler's name and address appear on the outside and inside of each checked bag, and (2) verify after check-in that the agent has given you the right number of claim tags for the bags you checked, and that each of them show the correct destination.

Lost and misrouted bags are a problem you must anticipate. In the last two years, five out of seven mission trips I have taken on British Airways from the U.S. to Budapest culminated in at least one team member's bag not arriving with the group on each trip. If your luggage is missing, be sure you file a claim before you leave the airport and ask the airline to telephone you to update the errant bag's progress.

If your final destination is in the same country as the arrival airport, you can insist the airline delivers the bag to you, free. If you are using surface transportation to travel to a third country, most airlines abdicate their responsibility to deliver the bags to you. When you fly into Budapest, then bus the team to Moldavia, the airline would have you make the twelve-hour round-trip drive to Budapest the next day to retrieve the bag they misplaced. Plan ahead: If there is a lost bag, you might delegate a team leader *pro tem* to go with the group while you remain in Budapest, hopefully only until the next flight a few hours later. There have been times when the airline has given misleading information, and the bags did not arrive for five days. You must make it clear to the owner of the lost bag that you are not delivering an ironclad promise of arriving with the missing luggage. Remember, although the airline will not offer it to you, they will usually pay for incidentals, toiletries, etc.—but you are on your own for the hotel and meals while you wait for the bag to arrive. If you volunteer for such an assignment, make sure you hold onto the ticket and baggage claim check of the bag's owner, along with a signed note authorizing you to pick it up.

Lost Passports

Well ahead of the team's departure from home, I suggest team leaders ask their members for a photocopy of their passport pages that contain the photograph, signature, document number, issue date, birth date, and other data. This serves two purposes. First, you can personally verify that the passports will be valid at the time of travel. Second, you can have someone back home help in obtaining a replacement. You should make an extra copy of each passport data page; then take one set with you while leaving the second set at home with a reliable person you know you can always reach by telephone. If necessary, you can contact the person to exert pressure on the State Department to have a new passport issued overseas.

Caution your team members to treat passports and alien registration cards as more valuable than cash. Once, after realizing (on approach to New York), that the Alitalia agent in Rome had not returned my Green Card to me after checking in nine hours earlier, the U.S. Immigration officer told me the going black market rate for such documents was $10,000. "It's probably already been sold," he said. So if you ever meet an illegal alien called

Dave Forward, making dough in the back room of a pizzeria in Little Italy, call immigration!

Back to the serious matter of a lost passport. Do not report it until an exhaustive search has been completed. Once reported lost, it cannot be easily "unreported." However, once you have looked under the bus seat, in the hidden bag pocket, and through the dirty blue jeans and realize it is gone, you must contact the U.S. Embassy or Consulate immediately. (There is only one embassy in a country—in the capital city. Consulates may be found in large regional towns.)

Team leaders should have the telephone numbers of the nearest U.S. Embassy or Consulate for every area through which their group will travel. You can obtain these contacts by calling the U.S. Department of State in Washington, D.C., at 202-647-4000. The embassy staff will instruct you on the current procedures for issuing a replacement passport. Remember, until your team member is in possession of a valid passport, he cannot leave the country he is in. Their failure to return on their scheduled ticketed flight could also result in them being charged the full, nondiscounted fare home—often triple what they already paid. Arrangements for a replacement passport should be initiated without delay.

Legal Trouble Abroad

Sometimes there is a thin line between legitimate fines and bribery—in any country. I have seen border guards insist on a $50 cash payment for a "fuel fee" to cross the frontier when no such charge officially existed. I have three times been stopped and had the traffic policemen demand cash on the spot.

However, what if a team member experiences a more serious brush with the law? In a traffic accident, for example, even if you were not at fault, many countries place the primary fault on the foreigner. The team leader should contact the U.S. Embassy immediately. Knowing the name of the current American ambassador to that country is important. The moment will come when an official senior enough to make a release decision (and who probably understands English) will become involved. When you firmly tell him that Mr. B—(your ambassador's name) was expecting you to be treated well and that this officer's actions could cause an international incident, he might back off.

Nothing I am saying here is meant to belittle or excuse blatant violations, such as illegal narcotics handling, for which most foreign countries have the severest punishment imaginable. The preceding advice is given for those incidents where a local official gets a little carried away and thinks he can scare the "rich Americans" into a bribe. You should not delay in calling the closest U.S. Embassy or Consulate, or your home-based contact can call the State Department number for U.S. citizens in trouble overseas (202-647-5225).

The U.S. government will provide names of local English-speaking attorneys to assist. They will not pay fines, bail money, or defense costs.

BAD BEHAVIOR

It should not be surprising that some team members may at times engage in bad behavior while on the mission. The stress is great in a different culture, and some respond in ignorance or in seeming retaliation. Remember Rosa (chapter 9), who made many unwise decisions and almost undermined one mission trip? One way to discourage such action and remind members of their responsibility to the team is to have them agree to a covenant.

Have Members Sign the Covenant

One of the first things all team members should do when they commit to the mission trip is complete and sign a covenant and release of claim form, in which they agree to certain behavior, and to act in the team's interests (see sample in Appendix A). This document clearly establishes the team leader's authority. He should carry copies of each covenant with him during the trip. If an individual misbehaves, the team leader must determine the cause; the misbehavior may be just the excitement of the adventure, a cultural misstep, or an independent action on the member's part. If you're the leader, ask yourself what the consequences are. Could their behavior harm people? Could their actions damage the mission work of the team and the career missionaries? You can probably nip the problem in the bud by just talking privately with the offender. You do not need to be authoritarian or carry a big stick. Just ask them if they understand the implications of their gaffe and try to elicit from them a promise that it will not happen again.

If the behavior continues to the extent that other team members notice and are disturbed by it, the problem needs to be addressed at a team meeting. The team leader might find it helpful to privately ask a couple of those who have complained to voice their concerns when the individual is present. Open and close the meeting with prayer, and ask the people to also say something positive about the individual whose actions they are also criticizing. Note the distinction of criticizing the behavior, not the person.

The ultimate conclusion, reached only after serious and prayerful determination that the person's actions are endangering the project or the lives of those working on it, is to send the member home. That is not always easy, especially if the person is a teen away from home or has a nonchangeable airfare in a destination halfway around the world. The cost and inconvenience is great. Furthermore, it will probably cause repercussions back home and should only be considered when all other options have failed.

Sometimes the misbehavior comes after personality conflicts deteriorate. The apostle Paul, writing to the church in Corinth in advance of his third trip there, feared that the mutual excitement leading up to his visit could degenerate into the same human failings we experience today. Quarrels, anger, and even slander can occur, even when we gather as a group of Christians with the finest motives: "I am afraid that when I come I may not find you as I want you to be . . . ," the apostle admits. "I fear that there may be quarreling, jealousy, outbursts of anger, factions, slander, gossip, arrogance, and disorder" (2 Corinthians 12:20).

Do Not Ignore Bad Behavior or Personality Conflicts

If you are the team leader, do not ignore either bad behavior or persistent infighting among the group. Choose the "easy" way and ignore a pair of team members who stay out late after dinner each night, and you will soon discover that the remaining members get angry with you—for not enforcing the rules to which everybody had agreed, and which apply to the whole team. On other occasions, you can quietly ask people who have personality clashes with each other to stay clear of their antagonist if they could simply find no other common ground. If the problem continues, it needs to be publicly aired at a team meeting.

You need look no further than the words of our Lord to establish the foundation for resolving such ill will. Matthew 18: 15–20 serves as an excellent platform from which to settle conflicts and mediate disputes. Look also at Jesus' statement as found in Matthew 5:21–24 (TLB):

> "Under the laws of Moses the rule was, 'If you kill, you must die.' But I have added to that rule, and tell you that if you are only angry, even in your own home, you are in danger of judgment! If you call your friend an idiot, you are in danger of being brought before the court. And if you curse him, you are in danger of the fires of hell. So if you are standing before the altar in the Temple, offering a sacrifice to God, and suddenly remember that a friend has something against you, leave your sacrifice there beside the altar and go and apologize and be reconciled to him, and then come and offer your sacrifice to God."

Those are wise and worthy words for all team leaders to remember!

MUTUAL RESPONSIBILITIES

One team to Romania stayed in the dormitory attached to the home where the local lay mission field representative lived. Prior to arriving, the representative was described as the catalyst of all the mission successes in the region. When the team arrived in Romania on Saturday evening, after traveling eighteen hours, John came out and said, "Welcome to Romania!" Then he left, and for two days the team leader had to negotiate with John's wife, Angela, to make the arrangements they had already agreed to by phone and fax months earlier. On Tuesday, word came back that John was too busy to make the specific arrangements some team members had come expressly to perform. Members of the construction team could not work at the church and orphanage building site they had come to help build because, as they told the team leader, "We ran out of cement and have no money to buy more."

The group then gave Angela $600 in cash—enough, she

said, to buy an entire month's supply of cement—and elicited a promise that the team could work there the next day. On Thursday, however, the cement still had not arrived, and they sent the team to a pig farm and directed team members to dig a drainage ditch. On Friday, some cement arrived—at the pig farm—and John appeared before the team to thank them for coming to Romania. The team left six hours later.

We all have responsibilities. We have discussed many of our duties as individual participants' duties: be flexible, follow the rules, be considerate, act as Christians, be servant disciples, etc. The sending church or organization has a responsibility, too. Once its members approve the mission trip, they must support it with their prayers and whatever other resources they can muster to ensure its success. And the team leader is charged with the awesome responsibility of anticipating everything in advance, planning, training, leading, and helping form a cohesive team of the Lord's servants.

However, the hosts also have responsibilities, and in the above example, John and Angela (not their real names) clearly abdicated them. First, they *must* communicate their needs to the sending church. If the team leader writes that her group wants to build a chapel, or hold a VBS, the on-site mission professional should honestly answer the proposal. If the answer is no, the missionary should explain why: the community does not need a chapel, and there will be nine other VBS groups in the months before this team arrives. Then the missionary host should suggest what is really needed. The host should not paint overly optimistic pictures and build the team's expectations unfairly.

Once the host has agreed to the tasks the visiting team has proposed, he must do everything possible to make advance arrangements so the team can "hit the ground running." On that same frustrating trip, there were team members who for months had planned to work with the abandoned toddlers at an orphanage: they arrived to discover the local leaders had sent all the kids to foster homes in the country that week. The team included a pastor who had prepared as his contribution his expertise on church development with the area's untrained local pastors: he spent his time digging a trench at the pig farm. The team also had an anesthesiologist from a major university teaching hospital in the United States whose sole reason for making the trip was to teach her specialty to local doctors: she, too, left without so much as setting foot in a hospital or even meeting one local physician. They all came with John's knowledge and agreement—and lack of follow-through.

"Be flexible," may be Rule Number One, and indeed, the team members mentioned above were gracious and willing to be so. In any country, people forget to make arrangements, intentions are misunderstood, and situations change. Still, like those of us on the sending side, the receiving party must exercise great care to understand the reasons for the incoming teams, and try to make their investment of time, talents, and treasures worthwhile. In the case of John and Angela, for instance, they had a responsibility to follow through on the plans they had made and which they knew the team was planning to work on. When things did fall through the cracks, it was incumbent on Peter as the host to come to the team first, and say, "Plan A fell through, but here is where we really need aid; could you help us on Plan B?"

Two others ways John and Angela could have helped were by (1) honoring the $600 that was given specifically and solely to buy cement for the orphanage and church, and not decide arbitrarily to spend it on something else (that act alone violated a bond of trust which took a very long time to restore); and (2) being present for most of the short-term mission. John was a phantom figure to that work team. Team members spend thousands of their own dollars and their precious vacation time working on his project. He had the responsibility to spent some time with them. He could and should have shown them the work that was being done on his project and acted as if he were glad they were there. When they saw him coming and going throughout the week, yet without even acknowledging their presence, it sent a message that he did not care about them.

Try sending a letter to the field representative which details what you believe to be your mutual expectations and responsibilities. It is another step along that path of being bridge builders where we constantly strive to better understand each others' cultures and positions.

YOUR MINISTRY WHILE ONSITE

Ministry during the short-term missions project can range from construction to teaching. Here are some logistical items to consider in order to operate efficiently while on the missions trip.

If you are doing construction, consider what tools the team should bring. Are the voltage and wattage the same, and will the plug adapters and voltage converters handle the power for any electric tools you plan to take? Instead of buying new tools and equipment and taking them with you, why not help the local economy by buying them onsite? Also determine whether you want to leave the tools as gifts at the end of the project.

If you plan to teach songs in the local language, plan to explain their meaning in that language, too. Sometimes literal translations do not fit the melody, so after translating the words, show the finished version to a person fluent in the language before your team memorizes something that will not work.

How do you plan to convey your message to groups of adults, teens, and children? Items such as poster board, flip charts, and easels are virtually unobtainable in developing countries. Do you have a message that your team can deliver relatively free of props and which is simple to tell, without Western clichés? If you plan to operate vacation Bible schools, do you have sufficient craft or game supplies if far more children than you anticipate show up?

The local Christians with whom you work will eagerly introduce you to their families. Don't forget to take photographs of your own family, church, and community to help build those bridges of friendship.

KEEPING A JOURNAL

The short-term missions venture offers team members a unique and powerful ministry opportunity. It will not be repeated. Team leaders should urge their members to write a journal of their mission experience.

As a team member, you may never have kept a journal. Many of us lead such busy lives that we barely have time to accomplish our everyday priorities, let alone write a journal. But you are about to embark upon an experience that will remain with you for the rest of your life. It is sad how quickly we forget many details so soon after they occur as vivid, meaningful experiences. Team members who journal will often tell how many things they had forgotten, but which their journals brought back to them. Those precious moments, the cherished memories, are what will keep the dream of mission work alive in our prayers and actions, as well as in the prayers of our partners in mission in the years ahead.

Dozens of short-term missionaries have testified how glad they are that they (grudgingly, at first) agreed to keep a journal of their mission trip. Some started at the first planning meeting, and later shared with the team their early fears and concerns. Others have recalled the anniversary of their trip, and reread each day's entry on the same date but in later years. As a team leader, make journaling a requisite activity of your teams. Set aside time each day during the trip expressly for this purpose, and ask volunteers to read some of their entries with their team members at a couple of daily on-site team meetings. A list of journaling tips is included in Appendix B.

DAILY TEAM MEETINGS

Just as the team meetings were important before you left home, so are those you will hold every day during the trip—but for different reasons. On-site team meetings should not last more than thirty minutes and can be held any time of the day, although it seems to make sense to schedule them after a meal, since everyone is together then. You might rotate them between morning, midday, and evening times; or set them at the same time each day. One thing should never change however: attendance is mandatory. Team meetings during the trip have four great benefits: (1) to maintain morale and enthusiasm among the team and for the tasks to be done; (2) to update them on daily schedules, changes, news, etc.; (3) to build better disciples through devotional messages, music, and Bible readings; and (4) to discuss other matters that require team attention.

The Typical Meeting Agenda

Below is an agenda of a typical on-site team meeting. Afterward, I offer suggestions for several of the items.

Open with prayer
> Different member each day

Devotional or Scripture reading with brief thoughts on the reading
> Spiritual leader or different member each day

"Tell us about your day"
> Ask a representative of each task team to say what they did and share any thoughts or special moments from their activity

A reminder of what is planned next
> Team leader

Special announcements, sign-up sheets, etc.
> Team leader

Team-building exercise
> Everyone

Song or music
> Music leader

Other announcements

Closing prayer

This is a composite—do not try to do all this in one meeting! You can build on it for your own team, using various components throughout the trip at different gatherings. Here are some suggestions for several of the items.

Prayer

Ask the team member to be specific as she prays. If you met people with special needs today, the person can pray for them by name. If your group was blessed with something awesome: a work task finished ahead of time despite a rainstorm or children receiving Jesus as their Savior—express thanks for that experience. Make prayers meaningful and specific to this mission.

Scripture/Devotional Reading

If you announce before you leave home your intention of asking members to participate in a Scripture reading and bring a devotional thought, you will probably have more requests than you have meetings to hear them. If a pastor is coming along, ask him how he wants to handle this part of the meeting. Some feel it is their moment to use their training and experience to help team members grasp a better understanding of Scripture. Others are happy to share the moment with other team members. The Bible verses used in the predeparture training meetings can be used during the trip: they all specifically relate to world missions and the purpose for this adventure.

What's Happening Next?

Typically the on-site meeting will include a reminder of what's planned next. This is the time when you remind the group of such things as: "The van to construction site B leaves in twenty minutes—and don't forget to bring your water bottles and tool belt. Worship service tonight will be at First Baptist Church. We leave here *promptly* at 7:15. Don't forget to wear coats, gentlemen. Ladies, you need to wear skirts or dresses below the knee, and when we arrive, the men and women will sit on opposite sides of the aisle."

Team-Building Exercises

To paraphrase a familiar maxim, "The team that plays together and prays together, stays together." Although the purpose for these trips is very serious, we sometimes need to loosen up and have fun while doing it. One such exercise to try to introduce at an early on-site team meeting is "My most embarrassing moment." The meetings are not long enough to accommodate every team member, so approach a couple of people and ask them to share their funny stories when you bring the topic up, then throughout the trip you can ask for additions as other members recall their anecdotes.

Remember, one important purpose of the meetings is to build up the confidence and motivation for missions of the team members. At the end of a week when they have worked tirelessly, lived in conditions they are not used to, and come together as a team, I like to conduct a final exercise. It builds self-esteem and goodwill that I have been told stays with them for years. First, I provide each person with same number of "comment slips" as there are team members. Then each person is handed an envelope and asked to print his or her own name on it. Each person then passes his or her envelope to the person on the right. That person is then asked to write on the first slip of paper some positive reflection about the team member whose envelope they have; then he or she inserts the paper in the envelope. When all are done, we pass each envelope again to the right and repeat the process. This continues until each envelope is returned to its owner. The envelope, now filled with positive affirmations, reminds the member about what a difference he or she has made to the team.

SOME FINAL CONSIDERATIONS

While in the host country, you are the guest. As we discussed in chapter 9, part of your effective Christian witness and good communication involves culturally sensitivity. Here are some final suggestions for being cultural sensitive, as well as ideas for dealing with transportation issues while in the country. We begin with the dos and then move to the don'ts.

- Remember that when you are in a foreign country, you are the foreigner.
- Do bring house slippers if you will be staying in people's homes and they have a carpet. It is considered rude in many cultures to wear shoes inside the house. Furthermore, a vacuum cleaner is often beyond the means of most families. Look at your host: does he have his shoes on? Try to follow that example.
- Do speak slowly, but not more loudly. Volume will not help a foreign national understand you. Speaking slowly, enunciating your words clearly, and avoiding idioms and slang will.
- Do recognize that personal cleanliness standards are different in some cultures. Some of the dearest people have a strong body odor because they are simply not used to bathing as regularly, nor using deodorant as fastidiously as we do. When we realize that the people Jesus visited, prayed, and dined with probably also had similar bathing habits, we can easily see that if it did not bother Him, who are we to make nasty comments about our hosts?

- Be prepared for rental vehicles overseas not to be equipped with what we consider standard accessories. Air-conditioning, automatic transmissions, radios, and tape players are reserved only for true luxury cars in most countries.

- Ask yourself how you would deal with a missed flight connection or other dilemma and jot down some battle plans in advance when your mind is clear.

- Do not use American terms when speaking to locals, or when speaking in public and you are using a translator. Instead of referring to something as "a mile long," or "scoring a touchdown," translate it into "1.6 kilometers," and "scoring a goal."

- Do not call another currency "funny money," nor be tempted to ask, "How much is that in real money?"

- Do not yield to the temptation to help a local person obtain a U.S. visa. It is extremely difficult to secure one, especially for nationals of developing countries. The statement made with the best of intentions that you will write to your member of Congress can produce hopes in the local citizen that are often dashed later.

- Do not take a local person's name and address unless you really do intend to write to the person. Most residents of the host communities are simple folk, with few friends outside their village. When they think they have befriended someone from across the world who will become their pen pal, they are proud and happy. That excitement can be crushed when you are too busy in your everyday life back home to respond to (or even understand) their letters.

- Do not refer to people in your host country as driving on the "wrong" side of the road if they drive on the left. When you do drive in developing nations, plan ahead for such eventualities as flat tires and mechanical problems. What would be a thirty-minute response from your auto club back home can be an all-day adventure in some areas. One team whose vehicle ran out of gas in Moldavia had to wait for fuel to be brought across the border from

Ukraine! What would you do if that happened to your team? By thinking it through ahead of time, the team leader in Moldavia suggested they visit the nearby village and visit with the surprised residents. Six hours later, the "stranded" team members had new friends they didn't want to leave. Only after prying the huggers apart could the journey be resumed. "What a privilege to share our Christian love and prayer," one team member remarked.

Chapter Twelve

✳

AFTER YOUR RETURN

*Y*ou have been through all the emotions: excitement over the trip of a lifetime, concern over your ability to contribute, compassion for disparate needs, and, finally, gratitude for what the Lord has blessed you with. In the space of a week or two, you have felt a closer bond with God than ever before and had what many call a "life-changing experience." Now you come home to air-conditioning, stores stocked with abundance, and a society which lives in opulence compared to what you have just witnessed. It's time for a new set of emotions: sadness, guilt, anger . . . So how can you put your experience into perspective so that you fulfill your original objective of building the kingdom of God?

If you are the mission team leader, it is essential that you learn from this experience so that future groups can look forward to even greater success. The best way to do this is to ask the participants to evaluate the mission. If you are a team member, this evaluation will help you put your experience in perspective, and remind you of what God has done and can do in your life.

The team probably has a fairly long journey home from the mission site. Never will their experiences be fresher in their minds than now. The leader should provide a preprinted evaluation form, such as Form 3 shown in Appendix A, to each person and ask members for their honest opinions on a variety of important issues. Be specific. Don't ask a lot of closed questions that they can answer with a yes or no. Ask open questions that require them to think about a response and then provide it in narrative form. (Avoid a roundtable discussion upon their return; you run the risk of some people dominating the discussion while others feel too shy or intimidated to speak.)

Ask questions that reflect on the trip (How would you consider the value and efficiency of the travel arrangements?), along with some that focus on the future: "What specific suggestions do you have for improving our evangelism outreach on future short-term mission trips?" You can ask that the forms be signed or left anonymous, but request that they be returned to you before arrival home to avoid their being misplaced in the maelstrom of unpacking and family reunions.

As a participant, this is your opportunity to help not only your leader but yourself to understand some ways God has challenged and helped you as a follower of Jesus Christ. In addition to evaluating the trip, be sure to complete the "Personal Application" form (Form 4 in Appendix A), which will help you to share what you learned with others and focus anew on praying for missionaries and strengthening your devotional life.

As a leader reading the evaluations later, be aware that seemingly negative comments are not directed personally at you; even if a few are, you know from your servant-disciple training that none of us can expect to be perfect.

After arriving home from a mission trip, experiencing a letdown feeling is usual for the individuals. Team leaders can help participants combat those anticlimactic emotions. The first step is to address them up front. Tell the team that they may experience the missionary's equivalent of buyer's regret once the excitement and adventure of the trip have passed. Warn them not to expect their family and friends to be as excited about their mission experience as they are. With married couples it can even be worse than that: while one spouse was meeting new people, running Vacation Bible School and excitedly trying out new language skills on his eager hosts, the partner at home had to deal with the children alone, a broken water pipe, and a medical emergency with the baby.

Do warn the team not to broadcast the negative incidents from the trip. Human nature being what it is, the snafus or personal missteps are likely to be remembered by those back home long after they have forgotten all the good your team accomplished. Such publicity can only hurt future mission support.

THE TEAM LEADER'S THANK-YOU NOTE

At one of the last on-site meetings, go around the room asking each member to share what has been his or her most rewarding experience during the mission. As the person speaks, take a few notes. Then as the trip is ending, write personal notes to all team members and mail it to their home addresses. Knowing that it will take two to four weeks to arrive, you can thank members for the contribution of their time and talents, and tell them how much their work has meant to the host community. If possible, include some reference to the points they made about their own sense of personal accomplishment. What a meaningful moment it will be when they receive your note several weeks later, recognizing their contributions and telling them that they did make a difference—just when the anticlimactic feelings are at their peak.

REPORTING TO THE CONGREGATION

When two of our earliest missionaries—Barnabas and Paul—returned from their first overseas mission trip, "they gathered the church together and reported all that God had done through them and how he had opened the door of faith to the Gentiles" (Acts 14:27). Paul knew about the importance of communicating the success of his mission back then, and it is a no less pressing imperative for us today.

If you have several people from the same church, ask the pastor for a "moment for mission" at a worship service (or even a major part of the service) soon after your return. The congregation has been following and supporting this mission for months, both financially and in prayer. This is an ideal opportunity to let them see how those prayers have been answered, and how meaningful their support has been to the missionaries and those they served. Instead of the usual team leader's "talking head" presentation, ask each team member to present a brief testimony about their work and sense of fulfillment. Then you might teach the congregation one of the foreign language songs the team learned.

Arranging a mission supper, with foods indigenous to the area to which you traveled, crafts you purchased, and slides or video of the team in action, is another excellent way of communicating to the congregation the value of your team's work. At the same time, it can become a springboard for the next mission team. Your short program can serve as a "commercial" to promote interest in the next short-term mission trip.

THE TEAM REUNION

Another highlight of any short-term mission is the team reunion, best scheduled three to four weeks after their return. It might be an activity the team can plan; the team leader can sit back and be the guest at this event! After preparing, traveling, living, eating, and working together, the reunion is the opportunity to relive some of those wonderful moments the team experienced together. It also serves to bring closure to the experience. Ideally held as a covered-dish picnic at the home of a centrally located team member, you should invite spouses, parents of youth participants, and anyone who has endured the months of preparations of the team members.

Activities might include asking each team member to:

- Share one entry from his journal
- Describe what was the most meaningful part of the trip
- Illustrate how her life will be changed because of the experience
- Tell about something God enabled him to do that he did not think he could do
- Describe her relationship with Jesus Christ before and after the trip

The reunion can serve as the forum for a final rendition of the songs the team learned and for the team leader to issue one final journal assignment: "What is next? Where do I go from here to better support mission work?"

The reunion is also a great opportunity to share each other's photographs, and you should anticipate how you will deal with those requests. One way is to have the rolls developed with a second set of prints, which you can give out at random. Many discount photo finishers now offer the second set of prints free.

Instead of squinting at dozens of tiny negatives to order reprints, mark the back of each print with a code. Be sure to use a pen that will not transfer ink onto the next print. Here is an easy code format: The first two digits represent the year. The second two, the month. The third two, the roll number. The final two digits are the print number. If you take ten rolls of film during a trip in August 1997, you will assign the first set of prints you catalog as roll number 01. You would thus number the first print in that set 97-08-01-01. On the back of the last print in that roll of twenty-four photographs, you would write 97-08-01-24. The first print in the second roll would be numbered 97-08-02-01, and so on. When people ask for reprints, just ask them to give you a note with their name and the codes from the pictures they want. If you use the new Advance Photo System (APS), each roll comes with a code number, and the film processor prints that code with the date and negative number on the back of each photograph, so your work is done for you.

Those warm memories are nice, but the real joy as you gather comes in knowing you and other team members have had an impact for Christ through the mission. And, as we will see in the conclusion, that impact can be lasting, affecting people for eternity as you strengthen and empower believers as well as bring unbelievers to saving faith in Jesus.

CONCLUSION

This *Guide* has noted the many benefits that come from short-term missions. We have read of how short-term mission work helps people in need, spreads the Gospel, and raises to new heights the giving and church involvement of participants. Beyond the practical advice and "how-to" mechanics of developing effective teams, the *Guide* has reminded us of the real joy of serving the Lord by sharing our talents in a mission setting.

Could there be a downside to this church-wide trend of emphasizing short-term missions? "Short-term ministry is a problem only when people go unprepared," advises Elizabeth Lightbody, missions professor at Moody Bible Institute and former short-term missions coordinator (for ten years) with SEND International.

As you prepare for your missions trip, here are three contemporary concerns you and your team should be alert to as you enter another culture with the Gospel. An awareness of these issues will make your short-term mission preparation and service more effective.

DEPENDENCY VERSUS EMPOWERMENT

Without careful planning and forethought, the well-intentioned mission team comes home feeling personally rewarded while leaving no mechanism in place for their work to be continued in their absence.

One team spent two weeks evangelizing in Kazakhstan, a former republic of the Soviet Union. Team members did a great job, having taught more than a thousand children in vacation Bible schools and four times that number at evangelism meetings in a dozen towns. The team returned home glowing with feelings of great accomplishment, eager to tell about the people who had accepted Christ and the experiences they had witnessed.

Yet they had acted independently of any local church or mission agency, giving no thought to how the good work they had started would be continued after they returned home. "We plan to return next year," explained the group leader enthusiastically. Maybe so, but how effective a ministry were they establishing when the people they served would see them only once a year? By making them wait for the American church team's plane to land before Kazakhstan's new Christians could receive news of God's Word, the mission team had made them dependent on the annual short-term trek.

How much more effective would these well-intentioned folks have been if they had established a partner relationship with the local church or missionaries? By working with the indigenous Christian leadership, they could have empowered those people to achieve a far more effective ministry, working to strengthen the bonds of faith and fellowship they had helped forge. The difference, which they should have planned for months before the team left home, could have been made if they had viewed themselves as supporters of the Christians in the field, rather than adopting their "go it alone" attitude. The goal should have been to empower the very people who know best the local culture—the pastors and Christians who live there—to grow spiritually and evangelize their own people. Similarly, we should help the local missionaries who will remain after our departure, whose knowledge, language skills, and very presence mean they are committed and highly prepared to winning the local souls for Christ.

SHORT-TERM VERSUS CAREER MISSIONARIES

Many mainline denominations have experienced a minor revolution in recent years. Local congregations, perhaps influenced by the political trend to reduce the waste and abuse of central government spending, frequently perceived their money sent to church headquarters as unwisely allocated. One reason short-term missions have become so popular is that participants feel a greater sense of accomplishment and enthusiasm when they experience the work personally, compared to mailing a check to headquarters.

Sadly, this diversion of financial resources has hurt both long-term mission support and the career missionaries in the field. "Why do so many congregations assume they must see missions firsthand before they will give? Why do they need to see videos of themselves on location before they care about missions?" asked *Christianity Today* in a December 1996 editorial.

Indeed, although changes in the way career missionaries take the Gospel to the field have been necessary, the fact remains that long-term mission work is as imperative today as it ever was. William Carey, the English shoemaker who founded his country's first missionary society before going to India in 1794 as a missionary, is known as "the father of modern missions." For all Carey's tireless work in the field, it took six years for the first Indian convert to accept Christ. Today, most short-termers (and many headquarters-types who oversee career missionaries) would consider such a timeline utter failure. Yet Carey knew his mission was measured in decades, not weeks. Despite the "slow" start, by the time of his death in 1834, Carey had used his forty years of mission service to:

- Translate the Bible into three languages and forty dialects.
- Help convert more than 15,000 Indians to Christianity.
- Start dozens of churches.
- Found ninety-two Christian schools and the largest seminary in India.

• Inspire and help train fifty-eight new missionaries—including two of his sons—to spread the Gospel throughout India.

Without question, the ongoing ministry of career missionaries is invaluable. As short-termers, we must view ourselves as their partners, assisting them for a brief period in their ongoing lifework of missionary service. A good example of today's trend toward partnering short-termers and career missionaries occurred in Kenya recently. For eight weeks during their summer college break, a youth mission team from Pasadena, California, aided a local missionary. Several youth walked door-to-door, meeting every family in the area. Other team members visited the schools and fields to talk with the children and men. They asked questions about their families and their worship habits, and members handed them custom-printed materials.

Each week the team helped the mission field worker with Bible studies held for women, men, children, and families. Each week the attendance grew, with the visitors exchanging hugs and handshakes with the young people they had met at their homes. Early in their mission the members had met with the career missionary to learn about his work, seeking and adhering to his advice. Jointly the missionary and the short-termers had set strategy and goals. By the time the mission team returned home, the field worker had a core group of 150 villagers who committed to Christ and to worshiping regularly at the open-air church. The team departed with an enormous sense of accomplishment and supportive feelings for future missions and deep respect for the missionary's gifts and commitment. The missionary saw his work magnified in ways he alone could never have achieved.

Writing in *International Bulletin of Mission Research* in January 1995, Robert Coote said:

> In a world where hundreds of millions have yet to hear the name of Christ and additional millions have never heard the gospel presented effectively in their cultured context, there is no substitute for the career missionary. One can take only limited satisfaction in reports of uncounted thousands of short-termers engaged in missions . . . [but they] cannot balance a real decline in long-term commitments by men and women who are prepared to take a pro-

foundly incarnational approach to communicating the gospel of Jesus Christ to people of other cultures.[1]

It is important that we use short-term mission work to complement—not to compete with—that of career missionaries and long-term support programs. Short-termers often return from a mission trip moved by the experience and ready to share their enthusiasm with anyone in the congregation who will listen. We need to channel that energy and communicate it to support the work of medium- and long-term mission workers so that they increase financial and prayer support for all missions.

DO NO HARM

In chapter 9 we considered the issue of cultural sensitivity. We must provide our mission teams with proper cross-cultural training and the wisdom to understand that they cannot transplant their hometown ways into a foreign environment. Career missionaries, and even medium-termers, receive lengthy training in the culture of their host communities. The unprepared "tourists for Jesus," who go into a community determined to change the world in a week can actually do more harm than good, warns Miriam Adeney, associate professor of cross-cultural ministries at Seattle Pacific University. How so? Remember Rosa? Similarly, Stefan inadvertently offended a local pastor and undermined that pastor's credibility and the trust of his teenagers when he wore an earring without thinking (or inquiring).

A mainline denomination that practices open Communion at home sent a mission team to Romania. The entire team celebrated Communion during the trip and invited the local Christians they had met to join them. They were unaware that it was a huge cultural gaffe to invite teens to participate in the sacrament.

Remember also that being culturally sensitive means respecting the people and rejecting our subtle biases. "Too often we swoop down to clean up a disaster at the bottom of a cliff when we ought to be helping the people build a fence across the top," Adeney says. "We should stop and ask: Why are so many people sick? Poor? Uneducated?"[2] Viewing a local community in Mexico or Appalachia or Africa or south-central Los Angeles from the insularity of our home-church mission committee can make that a very difficult question to answer. But pose it to our partner, the on-site career mission worker, and we can more objectively understand the bigger picture. Then we can decide how to truly act as good stewards of our time, talent, and treasures to solve those needs.

Having devoted the foregoing chapters to the benefits and joy of participating in short-term mission work, I believe a few cautionary words in this conclusion are important. Remember that nothing you do once onsite can outweigh the importance of preparations made while still at home. Digging beneath the superficial stratum of general information on your host community to understand fully *why* you are going, *whom* you are going to see, and *how* you can develop servant relationships to assist— rather than drain—mission specialists in the field is critical.

Training participants in cross-cultural knowledge, from language skills to how to dress and where to sit in church, cannot be overemphasized. As Stephen Covey urges in his best-selling *Seven Habits of Highly Effective People*: "Seek first to understand, then to be understood."[3] Try to understand the culture, traditions, history, politics, the trials, strengths, and faith journeys of the people in your host community before you set foot in their midst.

THE BIGGER PICTURE

Bear in mind that despite your most carefully planned mission team, the local community (and probably missionaries and church leader partners) have been in place long before you arrive and will be there long after you leave. By viewing those in the host destination as partners in God's overall plan for the world, we can realize results barely imagined a few years ago. Korean and African churches are now sending their own missionaries to unreached people groups around the world. New Christians in Romania and Bulgaria are taking the Word into Albania. And after years of sending short-term mission teams to establish churches in Costa Rica, First Presbyterian Church of Bethlehem, Pennsylvania, now partners with their Costa Rican brothers and sisters to jointly send teams to Pakistan. We *are* winning the world for Christ!

Seeing your contributions as one tiny part of the whole long-term solution can remove much of the stress that teams experience when they try to accomplish too much during their stay. When incorporated into your daily commitment to pray for that world vision of mission success through self-sacrifice, servant-discipleship, and improved intercultural understanding, it is a vision that cannot fail to come true!

With proper preparations; with the paradigm of short-term missions perhaps refocused slightly after reading this book; with the abilities of your well-chosen team and the strength and joy that comes from serving Jesus Christ by serving your needy brethren, you are on your way to changing the world!

Why are so many Christians discovering short-term mission work today? Is it because they are following the direct order of Christ Himself? Is it because through this activity they can help the needy and bring new souls into the family of believers? Could it be because the Holy Spirit spoke to them and motivated them to become involved? Is it because they can give up a week or two of their vacation time for an experience which brings them closer to Jesus and His people? The answer is a resounding yes!

Forget the statistics. Don't worry about the minor logistics. The solitary young woman you get through to in Albania could go on to be the next Mother Teresa. The young translator who saw the lifesaving work your medical team was able to accomplish may have decided to go on to become a doctor herself to help her fellow citizens in the future. That kid you played—and prayed—with in Guatemala could be a future Latino Billy Graham. One life you touch may be as profoundly changed as those of the simple folks our Lord touched, and who went on to be His most precious disciples.

What a privilege it is to use our vacation time to carry the Gospel into the world so that on that great promised day we will see " . . . a great multitude that no one could count, from every nation, from all tribes and peoples and languages, standing before the throne and before the Lamb" (Revelation 7:9 NRSV). May God be with you in the planning and execution of your adventure in short-term missions.

NOTE

1. Robert Coote, "Good News, Bad News: North American Protestant Overseas Personnel Statistics in Twenty-five Year Perspective," *International Bulletin of Mission Research* 19 (January 1995): 6.
2. Miriam Adeney, "McMission," *Christianity Today*, 11 November 1996, 14.
3. Stephen R. Covey, *The Seven Habits of Highly Effective People* (New York: Simon & Schuster, 1989), 235.

SUGGESTED READING

Anthony, Michael J. *The Short-term Missions Boom*. Grand Rapids: Baker, 1994.

Barrett, David B. *World-Class Cities and World Evangelization*. Birmingham, Ala.: New Hope, 1986.

Borthwick, Paul. *A Mind for Missions*. Colorado Springs: NavPress, 1987.

Bryant, David. *In the Gap*. Madison, Wisc.: InterVarsity, 1979.

Burns, Ridge. *The Complete Student Missions Handbook*. Grand Rapids: Zondervan, 1990.

Campolo, Anthony, Jr. *The Success Fantasy*. Wheaton, Ill.: Victor, 1980.

Dillion, William P. *People Raising*. Chicago: Moody, 1993.

Eaton, Chris and Kim Hurst. *Vacations with a Purpose*. Elgin, Ill.: Cook, 1993.

Fuller, Millard. *No More Shacks!* Waco, Tex.: Word, 1976.

Hancock, Jim. *Compassionate Kids*. Grand Rapids: Zondervan, 1996.

Hesselgrave, David J. *Communicating Christ Cross-Culturally*. 2nd ed. Grand Rapids: Zondervan, 1991.

Hiebert, Paul G. *Anthropological Insights for Missionaries*. Grand Rapids: Baker, 1987.

Howard, David M. *The Great Commission for Today*. Downers Grove, Ill: InterVarsity, 1976.

Johnstone, Patrick. *Operation World*. Grand Rapids: Zondervan, 1993.

Jordan, Peter. *Re-Entry*. Seattle: YWAM, 1996.

Neill, Stephen. *A History of Christian Missions.* 2nd ed. New York: Viking, 1994.

Rumph, Jane. *Stories from the Front Lines.* Fairfax, Va: Chosen Books, 1996.

Sider, Ronald. J. *Rich Christians in an Age of Hunger.* Downers Grove, Ill.: InterVarsity, 1977.

Stott, John. *Christian Mission in the Modern World.* Madison, Wisc.: InterVarsity, 1976.

Wilson, J. Christy. *Today's Tentmakers.* Wheaton, Ill.: Tyndale, 1979.

Stepping Out: A Guide to Short-Term Missions, Seattle: YWAM, 1996.

World Christian Magazine, P.O. Box 40010, Pasadena, Calif. 91104.

SAMPLE TRIP FORMS

FORM 1

APPLICATION TO JOIN THE SHORT-TERM MISSION TEAM

This form is CONFIDENTIAL and will be used only to determine suitability for the team.

Team to: _____ Dates: _____

Sponsored by: _____

Your name: _____ Date of Birth: _____

Address: _____

Daytime tel: (____) _____ Evening tel: (____) _____

Your occupation: _____ Position: _____

Previous destinations you have visited on short-term missions: _____

Marital status: _____ Citizenship: _____

Passport No: _____

Languages spoken/degree of fluency: _____

Do you sing? _____ Instruments played:_____

T-shirt size: _____

Are you able to pay for this trip independently? _____

Anticipated scholarship assistance needed: $ _____

Why do you want to participate in this mission?

_____

_____

_____

_____

What do you hope to accomplish while on the trip?

_____

_____

_____

Are you a Christian? Do you feel Christ calling you to this mission trip?

_____

_____

_____

In what work area do you feel you can make the greatest contribution?

_____

_____

_____

What are some of your concerns over joining this team?

_____

_____

_____

Please describe any medical condition that a doctor might need to know of during the trip:

_____

_____

_____

What prescription medications do you take (generic name, strength, and frequency of dosage):

_____

_____

_____

_____

_____

What is your blood type? _____ Are you pregnant? _____ Due: _____

Please describe your general health condition:

_____

_____

_____

Please list any known allergies:

_____

_____

_____

Please describe briefly the dates and results of any problems encountered with:

Hypertension _____

Heart Attack or Heart Surgery _____

Hepatitis _____

Angina _____

HIV/AIDS _____

Stroke _____

What is your personal physician's name and telephone number?

_____

Has he or she, or any other medical professional, advised you not to participate in this or other short-term mission trips, or similar forays into Less-Developed Countries?

_____

In the event of an emergency, whom should we notify?

_____

Relationship: _____ Telephone: (____) _____

SOURCE: International Children's Aid Foundation. Used by permission. This form may be reproduced by team leaders for use in a short-term mission trip.

FORM 2

PERSONAL COVENANT & LIABILITY RELEASE FORM

The guidelines listed below are recommended for those participating in this journey. You go not as a tourist, but as a guest of another country. Romania is considered an LDC—Less Developed Country—and does not have the same conveniences you are used to at home. It is very important to be flexible and willing to adjust to the expectations of your host.

I recognize and accept the following conditions which will further the usefulness and safety of our short-term mission. If accepted as a member of this International Children's Aid Foundation team, I agree to:

1. Release and discharge the organizations and individuals which helped make these arrangements, including the International Children's Aid Foundation, [the sponsoring church—name of your church], their agents, employees, officers, and volunteers, from all claims, demands, actions, judgments, or executions that I have ever had, or now have, or may have, or which my heirs, executors, administrators, or assigns may have or claim to have, against these organizations, their agents, employees, officers, and volunteers, and their successors or assigns, for all personal injuries, known or unknown, and injuries to property, real or personal, caused by, or arising out of this journey. I intend to be legally bound by this statement.

2. Adopt an attitude that I am on this team to try to understand the host culture, not to convince them of my own viewpoint or style. I go knowing that there are many different ways to accomplish the same objective, and know that my way is not necessarily the best.

3. Abstain from making derogatory comments or arguments regarding people, politics, sports, religion, race, or traditions.

4. Go as a servant-disciple of Jesus Christ and will adopt that attitude when dealing with my fellow team members and the people I meet during the trip.

5. Accept and submit to the leadership role and authority of the team leader and promise to abide by his or her decisions as they concern this mission trip.

6. Acknowledge that by engaging in this journey, I am subjecting myself to certain risks voluntarily, including and in addition to those risks that I normally face in my personal and business life, including but not limited to such things as health hazards due to poor food and water, diseases, pests, and poor sanitation; potential danger from lack of control over local population; potential injury while working; and inadequate medical facilities.

7. Understand that our team's work is but a tiny speck on the bigger picture that our mission partners are trying to accomplish. I promise not to be overly demanding, to do my best not to offend or cause embarrassment for the local mission host, and to do my best to help them attain their long-term goals.

8. Attend all team meetings possible, both prior to departure and during the mission trip.

9. Expeditiously follow up on all requirements for passports, visas, financial obligations, vaccinations, travel insurance, etc.

10. Refrain from meddling, complaining, and obscene or insensitive humor. I realize that others on my team, during the journey, and while onsite will look at me for an example of how a Christian acts, and will not treat that responsibility lightly. I understand that travel, especially to remote locations, can be difficult, and I promise to adopt a flexible attitude and be supportive as plans may need to be changed. I understand that I must travel with the rest of the team, unless other prior arrangements are made.

11. Regard the differing styles of worshiping with respect. I promise that where I see the need, I will witness my faith, but without a superior, colonial attitude.

12. If a loved one or dear friend is traveling with me, we agree to interact with all members of the team, not just one another. I promise not to initiate or seek new romantic relationships with team members during the trip.

13. Avoid any actions which might be perceived as amorous attentions toward indigenous people I meet.

14. Refrain from using tobacco or alcoholic beverages while in the host country. Abstain from any illegal drugs or prohibited activity while on this trip.

15. Remember we are the new Christians from another part of the world and will be watched very closely. I will not take lightly this important responsibility of setting an example.

16. Refrain from giving gifts, such as money, clothes, jewelry, tape players, etc. Although the intent of the giver is good, the result after we leave has caused problems for our host, and jealousy and bitterness amongst those locals who received no such largesse. If I feel compelled to give a gift to someone I have met, I will consult first with the team leader before I promise or give the gift, and I promise to let him or her make the final decision on this matter. This covenant does not apply to the small fellowship tokens we will discuss and have approved before leaving home.

17. Act as a servant-disciple of the local pastor or mission organization. I will respect the advice I am given concerning attire, eating and drinking, and other such traditions which will help me to assimilate into the local community.

18. Understand that every member of this group is expected to share freely from their particular blessings and talents, whether that is skills such as music, art, carpentry, or basic hard work. I agree to participate in these ways as fully as possible.

19. I agree that in the event my conduct is considered so unsatisfactory that it jeopardizes the success of the trip, and that mediation during the trip has failed to correct my behavior, that my services in connection with this mis-

sion shall end and I shall return home immediately at my own expense.

20. In signing below, I represent that I am 18 years of age or older, or my parent/guardian will sign also, accepting the above conditions on my behalf.

Participant's Signature: _____

If participant is under 21 years of age, parent or legal guardian's signature:

_____

Participant's name: _____ (Please print)
Address: _____ (Please print)
Daytime phone: (____) _____
Evening phone: (____) _____

SOURCE: International Children's Aid Foundation. Used by permission. This form may be reproduced by team leaders for use in a short-term mission trip.

FORM 3

SHORT-TERM MISSION TRIP EVALUATION FORM

Name: _____ Date: _____

Country of Ministry: _____

1. Describe your most important objectives during the pre-trip planning stage.

   _____

   _____

   _____

2. What were your greatest concerns during the pre-trip planning stage?

   _____

   _____

   _____

3. What was the greatest lesson you learned during this mission trip?

   _____

   _____

   _____

4. What helped you learn this lesson? (Describe the experience, people, etc.)

   _____

   _____

   _____

5. What were the best parts of the overall experience?

   _____

   _____

   _____

6. How was the balance of work, fellowship, witnessing for you?

   _____

   _____

   _____

   _____

   _____

7. Which tasks were the most fulfilling for you?

_____

_____

_____

8. How would you describe the effect this trip had on your personal:
   a. Self image?

_____

_____

_____

   b. Spiritual life?

_____

_____

_____

   c. Interest in future missions?

_____

_____

_____

   d. God's overall plan for your life?

_____

_____

_____

9. Will you covenant to pray for any of the people with whom you worked?

_____

_____

_____

10. Do you plan to maintain contact with any of the people you met?

_____

_____

_____

11. Where do you rate yourself regarding missions service?

☐ I am definitely going to be a missionary or tentmaker

☐ I definitely want to return on another short-term mission trip

☐ I am open to being a missionary, but I am unsure where

☐ I just started thinking about being a missionary, and I am unsure where

☐ I am going to be a supporter of other missionaries

☐ I am opposed to the idea of missionary work

☐ I have never really thought about missionary work

12. What would be your biggest piece of advice concerning improving our teams in the future?

_____

_____

_____

13. Any general comments?

_____

_____

_____

14. On a scale of 1 to 5, 1 being "Very Bad" and 5 being "Excellent," please rate the following:

Travel arrangements	1	2	3	4	5
Team leadership	1	2	3	4	5
Pre-trip training	1	2	3	4	5
Host obligations met	1	2	3	4	5

Thank you for your participation and response

SOURCE: *Short-Term Missions Manual* of the Reformed Episcopal Church (Warminster, Pa.). Used by permission. This form may be reproduced by team leaders for use in a short-term mission trip.

FORM 4

PERSONAL APPLICATION OF WHAT I HAVE LEARNED

Name: _____

Read over your Journal and trip notes. What application are you going to make as a result of your short-term mission assignment?

1. Are you going to write to a missionary? Who? By when?

   _____

   _____

2. Are you going to read a missionary book? What? By when?

   _____

   _____

   _____

3. Are you going to tell friends about the team? Who? By when?

   _____

   _____

   _____

4. Are you going to speak in any classes at school, at work, or in church?

   _____

   _____

   _____

5. What ways are you going to grow in your devotional life?

   _____

   _____

   _____

6. What country (countries) will you try to learn more about so that you can pray for that country?

   _____

   _____

   _____

7. For whom are you going to be praying now?

_____

_____

_____

Who will hold you responsible to carry out these applications?

_____

(Give a completed copy of this form to that person)

SOURCE: *Short Term Missions Manual* of the Reformed Episcopal Church (Warminster, Pa.). Used by permission. This form may be reproduced by team leaders for use in a short-term mission trip.

Appendix B

✳

SAMPLE TRIP CHECKLISTS

JOURNALING CHECKLIST

What a Journal Is	Journaling Tips
A diary of daily thoughts & events	1. Start before you leave home
A record of my prayers & emotions	2. Set aside quiet time for writing
A way of preserving joy for the future	3. "Talk to it" as if it was your best friend
A list of daily priorities	4. Keep your journal confidential
A place for favorite sayings & quotes	5. Answer some questions in the entries:
A book for creative writing	• Where is God in my life right now?
Somewhere I can retreat to in peace	• What am I praying about?
My own history book	• Who did I meet today?
Where I can review my day with God	• What different things did I see today?
An exercise in self-discipline	• Include my interaction with the team
A record of answered prayers	• What work did I do today?
A blueprint for better future living	• What did I learn about serving Him?

PACKING CHECKLIST

✔	Item	✔	Item
	Bible		Stationery for thank-you notes to
	Dual language dictionary		send home
	First aid kit containing: cold		Personal tape player/tapes
	tablets, Tylenol, Band-Aids,		Spare batteries
	Kaopectate, hydrocortisone		Extra film
	cream.		Voltage/Plug converter
	Journal notebook		Gifts for hosts
	Only necessary credit cards		Insect repellent
	Phrase book		Sunscreen
	Wire clothes hangers		Spare eyeglasses
	Clothes pins, clothesline		Sunglasses
	Sewing kit with safety pins		Soap, shampoo, detergent
	Foldup raincoat/hat/umbrella		Family photos
	2 large towels, 2 washcloths		Work clothes/gloves
	Alarm clock (not electric)		Flip-flops (waterproof sandals)
	Address book		Place in carry-on bag:
	Toiletries		Motion sickness pills
	Toilet paper		Itinerary
	Bathrobe		Tickets
	Clothes/shoes for church		Passport
	MODEST swimwear		Prescription medication
	Luggage keys		Traveler's checks
	Money belt		Camera
	Spare pens		Cash
	Baggies for foreign currency		

TIP: Azusa Pacific University, which has a large student missions program to Mexico, provides packing checklists in Spanish—a real check of language skills before the team departs!

PASSENGER MANIFEST

A passenger manifest such as the example shown below (all names and numbers have been changed) can help the team leader maintain an easy overview of which items the participants have yet to supply (i. e., passport photocopies, or money still due).

Notice from this team how it stands out that one member has Canadian citizenship. That served as a red flag to check whether Canadians need visas for Romania, which, it turns out, they did.

Take several copies of the manifest with you. While on the trip, it serves as a checklist to see who is on the bus, etc. Also many border crossings and hotels are very pleased to be given a nice, legible list of the travel party.

ROMANIA MISSION TEAM – AUGUST 1996
PASSENGER MANIFEST
UPDATED 7/31/96

NAME	PASSPRT COPIES	PASSPORT #	SIT W/	MED INS	SHIRT SIZE	PHONE	PAID SO FAR
Forward, David C.	US ✔	571462582		✔	XL	988-1738	1500
Twomberg, David	US ✔	139443072	13	✔	XL	555-3569	1500
Anders, Jennifer	Canada ✔	*Needs VISA*B2856345	14	✔	L	555-9721	1200
Bidwell, Clara	US ✔	108111010	8	✔	XXL	555-1249	1200
Crest, Dr. Donald	US✔	619219644	6	✔	XL	555-1480	1400
Crest, Karen	US ✔	619719666	5	✔	XL	555-1480	1400
Jerrel, Dude	US ✔	736115382	9	✔	L	555-9044	1000
Light, Debbie	US ✔	112967736	4	✔	L	555-9753	1150
Might, Char	US ✔	168758816	7	✔	XL	555-6405	1000
Newson, Margaret	US ✔	1031601670	11	✔	L	555-7850	1200
Newson, Rev. Dan	US✔	1031901736	10	–	L	555-7376	1200
Scent, Rose	US ✔	9833659813	11	–	L	555-9620	1000
Warren, Mary	US ✔	845103568	3	–	M	555-7929	1100

TRIP CHECKLIST

A checklist should be given to all team members as a reminder of what to pack for their personal and team ministry needs. The following list was specifically for a team which was to provide medical care at a Christian clinic and child care at local orphanages.

ROMANIA TRIP CHECKLIST

For You	For the Clinic	For the Kids
Bible	Pain relievers	Diaper Rash cream
Travel insurance	Antihypertensives	/powder
U.S. currency	Allergy meds	Play parachute
Passport, Ticket	Antibiotics	Books in English for
Prescription meds, Spare	Surgical instruments	teens
glasses/contacts	Antacids, ulcer meds	Christian music tapes for
Nonprescr. lozenges,	Abdominal binders	teens
Tylenol, etc.		Christian T-shirts for
Journal		teens
Batteries		Baby soap, shampoo,
Ample film		brushes, combs, etc.
Voltage + plug converter		
Sanitary needs		
Toilet paper, Kleenex		
Deodorant, shampoo,		
etc.		
Snacks: granola bars,		
Crystal Light, etc.		
Pictures of family,		
church, community,		
US map		
Towels, soap, robe		
Small flashlight		
Reading materials		
Bug repellent, sunscreen		
Skirts, scarf for church		

Appendix C
SAMPLE TRIP ITINERARY

ROMANIA MISSION TEAM ITINERARY
AUGUST 1997

Fri. Aug. 9

Philadelphia International Airport, Terminal A . . . . . . .Check in . . . . .5:20 PM

British Airways BA 218, Boeing 747 . . . . .Depart . . . . . .7:20 PM

Dinner & Breakfast served aloft. Set watches
    ahead 5 hours before arrival in England.

Sat. Aug. 10

London Heathrow Airport, Terminal 4 . . . . .Arrive . . . . . . .7:25 AM
    (wait for team leader after aircraft exit),
    transfer to Terminal 1.

British Airways BA 868, Airbus A320 . . . . .Depart . . . . . . .10 AM
    A light lunch will be served aloft.
    Set watches *ahead* one hour before
    arrival in Hungary.

Budapest Ferighy Airport . . . . .Arrive . . . . . . .1:25 PM
    Our waiting bus will take us to Beius.
    Figure on about a six-hour trip.

    Set watches *ahead* one hour before crossing into Romania. Do not lose the tiny white *"Talon de Iesire"* form which the border guards will insert in your passport. If you cannot produce it when trying to exit Romania, you will experience extreme difficulty and delay. (But we promise to come visit you on our next visit to Romania.)

Sat. Aug. 17

Beius, Romania . . . . .Depart . . . . .5 AM

Set watches one hour *back* before crossing
    into Hungary.

Hotel Panorama, Budapest .Arrive. . . . . . .12 noon

211

Dinner at a local restaurant with Hungarian
  folk music . . . . .8:30 PM

Sun. Aug. 18

Hotel Panorama, Budapest . . . . .Depart. . . . . . .7:30 AM
Budapest Ferighy Airport, British Airways
BA 865, Boeing 757 . . . . .Depart . . . . .10 AM
Breakfast will be served aloft. Set watches
one hour *back* before arrival in England.
London Heathrow Airport, Terminal 1 . . . . .Arrive. . . . . .11 AM
  (wait for team leader after aircraft exit),
  transfer to Terminal 4.
British Airways BA 219, Boeing 747 . . . . .Depart. . . . . . .1:05 PM
Lunch and afternoon tea will be served aloft.
  Set watches 5 hours *back* before
  U.S. arrival.
Philadelphia International Airport, Terminal A . . . . . . .Arrive. . . . . .4 PM

Welcome home!

IMPORTANT NOTES

You are allowed two checked bags per person. Each bag may not weigh more than 70 pounds, nor exceed 62 dimensional inches (H+L+W). You are also allowed one carry-on bag, plus purses, umbrellas, cameras, etc.

Credit cards and traveler's checks are no good in Beius. Do not bring bills larger than $50, and make sure no banknotes have writing or ink on them. Bring several one-dollar bills. Upon arrival at Heathrow Airport, you might want to change a little money into British pounds, in case you want a buy a drink or newspaper during the two-hour layover. With Harrods and other great British stores located in the duty-free area of terminal 4, you definitely will not have to worry about unspent money on the return stopover! Change some money into Hungarian Forints upon arrival at Budapest airport. You'll need it when we stop for dinner en route to Romania, and to buy bottled water, etc., before we cross the border. If you change a maximum of $30, you'll still have lots left over for our night in Budapest on the way home. Tip: Bring small sealable plastic bags to keep separated the currencies of the three transit countries you are not presently in.

Relatives meeting you back in PHL may call BA for a flight check at 1-800-AIRWAYS.

In Beius, we will be staying with Peter & Ana Valaciu at 011 40 XXX-XXXX.

Calls from Europe are best made with a USA Direct-type calling card. Do not charge telephone calls back to the US to your hotel room. Surcharge of as much as 300 percent can result in a 10-minute call costing over $100! Instead, use your US telephone calling card and access your carrier by using their codes shown below. Here are the access numbers for the "Big Three":

	From England:	From Hungary:	From Romania:
AT&T	0500 89 0011	00*800 01 111	01 800 4288
MCI	0800 89 0222 or 0500 89 0222	00*800 01 411	01 800 1800
SPRINT	0800 89 0877 or 0500 89 0877	00*800 01 877	01 800 0877

* wait for second dial tone

Write down here the policy number and international telephone number of your travel insurance carrier: _____

Appendix D
✳
SAMPLE "MINIMUM LANGUAGE KNOWLEDGE" SHEET

Note: An excellent source of translation among thirty-two languages is the World Wide Web site http://www.travlang.com. For computers equipped with audio, it evens pronounces the words for you.

FRENCH

English	French	Phonetic
Hello/Good morning/ Good afternoon	Bonjour	*Bonn JURE*
Good evening	Bon soir	*Bohn SWAHR*
Good night	Bonne nuit	*Bun NWEET*
Goodbye	Au revoir	*Oh ruv-WAHR*
Yes/No	Oui/Non	*wee/gnaw*
My name is . . .	Je m'appelle	*Juh mop-PELL*
I am American	Je suis américain(m)/américaine(f) *Juh sweez ah-may ree-CAN/ ah-may-ree-KENNE*	
I am Canadian	Je suis canadien (m)/ canadienne(f) *Juh swee kah-nah-dee-YAN/ kah-nah-dee-YENNE*	
I am British	Je suis anglais (m)/anglaise(f) *Juh sweez on-glay/on-glez*	
I live in . . .	J'habite en (country)	*JaBEET on....*
	J'habite à (city)	*JaBEET ah...*
I am a Christian	Je suis chrétien(m)/chréteinne(f) *Juh sweez krayt-YAN/krayt-YENNE*	

215

English	French	Phonetic
Please/Thank you	S'il vous plait/Merci	*Seal voo PLAY/mare-SEE*
You're welcome	De rien	*Duh ree-YAN*
I am staying in . . .	Je reste à . . .	*Juh rest ah....*
I am on a Christian mission trip	Je voyage pour mission chrétien	
		Juh voy-AHGE poor mees-YON-krayt-YEN

0	1	2	3	4	5	6	7	8	9	10
zero	un	deu	trois	quatre	cinq	six	sept	huit	neuf	dix
zero	*unh*	*Duh*	*Twah*	*catruh*	*sank*	*SEEs*	*set*	*HWEET*	*nuf*	*DEEse*

SPANISH

English	Spanish	Phonetic
Hello	Hola	*OH-lah*
Good morning	Buenos dias	*Bweh-nohs DEE-az*
Good afternoon	Buenas tardes	*Bweh-nahs TAHR-dehs*
Good night	Buenas noches	*Bweh-nahs noh-chehs*
Goodbye	Adios	*Ah-dee-ohs*
Yes/No	Si / No	*See / Noh*
My name is . . .	Me llamo . . .	*May yah-moh . . .*
I am American	Soy estadounidense	*Soy ehs-tah-doh oo-nee-dehn-say*
I am Canadian	Soy canadiense	*Soy cah-nah-dee-ehn-say*
I am British	Soy Britanico/ca	*Soy bree-TAHN-ee-koh/-kah*
I live in . . .	Vivo en . . .	*Bee-boh ehn . . .*
I am a Christian	Soy cristiano/a	*Soy crees-tee-ah-noh/nah*
Please/Thank you	Por favor / Gracias	*Por fah-bohr / Grah-see-ahs*
You're welcome	De nada	*Day nah-dah*
I am staying in . . .	Me estoy quedando en . . .	*May ehs-toy kay-dahn-doh ehn*
I am on a Christian mission trip	Estoy en una excursion misionera cristiana	

Ehs-toy ehn oo-nah ex-coor-see-ohn mee-see-oh-nay-rah crees-tee-ah-nah

0	1	2	3	4	5
zero	uno	dos	tres	cuatro	cinco
zay-roh	*oo-noh*	*doss*	*trehs*	*kwah-troh*	*seehn-koh*

6	7	8	9	10
seis	siete	ocho	nueve	diez
seh-ees	*see-eh-teh*	*oh-cho*	*noo-eh-beh*	*dee-ehs*

ROMANIAN

English	Romanian	Phonetic
Hello	Salut	*SAI-oot*
Good morning	Buna dimineata	*BOO-na dee-men-YAT-sa*
Good afternoon	Buna ziua	*BOO-na ZEE-wa*
Good evening	Buna seara	*BOO-na see-ara*
Good night	Noapte buna	*Noo-AP-tay BOO-na*
Goodbye	La revedere	*La rev-a-DER-ray*
Yes/No	Da / Nu	*Daa / Noo*
My name is . . .	Numele meu este . . .	*NOO-mell-ay may-OO esta...*
I am American	Eu sunt american	*YEOO SOONtt aa-mer-ikaan*
I am Canadian	Eu sunt canadian	*YEOO SOONtt kaa-naa-de-aan*
I am British	Eu sunt britanic	*YEOO SOONtt brit-aan-eek*
I live in . . .	Eu locuiesc în . . .	*YEOO lockooy-EESK aan . . .*
I am a Christian	Eu sunt crestin	*YEOO SOONtt kresh-TEEN*
Please/Thank you	Te rog / Multumesc	*Te ROgg / MOOL-tzoo-mesk*
You're welcome	Cu placere	*COOP-la-cherrai*
I am staying in . . .	Eu stau la . . .	*YEOO staAO laa . . .*

I am on a Christian mission trip   Sant parte dintro echipa misionara crestina
SOONtt PAAR-tey DEEN-tro e-KEEP-er MEES-eon-AARa kresh-TEENa

0	1	2	3	4	5
zero	unu	doi	trei	patru	cinci
zero	*oonoo*	*doy*	*tray*	*pat-roo*	*cheench*

6	7	8	9	10
sase	sapte	opt	noua	zece
SHAr-seh	*SHArp-teh*	*opt*	*noow-eh*	*zech-ey*

LANGUAGE OF YOUR DESTINATION

English	Local language	Phonetic
Hello		
Good morning		
Good afternoon		
Good evening		
Good night		
Goodbye		
Yes/No		
My name is . . .		
I am American		
I am Canadian		
I am British		
I live in . . .		
I am a Christian		
Please/Thank you		
You're welcome		
I am staying in . . .		
I am on a Christian mission trip		

0   1   2   3   4   5

6   7   8   9   10

Appendix E

✳
SAMPLE SONG SHEET

Music makes for a powerful ministry, and you should use it both within your team and as you worship with your host community audiences.

It hardly demonstrates an attitude of "servanthood" if we go to another country, expecting them to know English. Your audiences will be very moved to notice you have made the effort to learn a few songs in their language.

This section includes several songs that are internationally known and also quite easy to learn in another language because they are repetitive. (Those listed with lyrics are in public domain.) They can be sung with the local citizens, such as during a Vacation Bible School, and by the team members during the daily on-site meetings. Find out in advance if there will be a musical instrument available for accompaniment. If not, make an audio tape of the music to these hymns before you leave home and take a small tape player with you.

You can purchase chorus books to leave with your hosts, but remember to obtain copyright permission before copying any words and music not in the public domain.

GOD IS SO GOOD
God is so good, God is so good, God is so good, He's so good to me.

He answers prayer, He answers prayer, He answers prayer, He's so good to me.

He cares for me, He cares for me, He cares for me, He's so good to me.

I love Him so, I love Him so, I love Him so, He's so good to me.

I'll praise His name, I'll praise His name, I'll praise His name, He's so good to me.

JESUS LOVES ME

Jesus loves me! This I know,
For the Bible tells me so;
Little ones to Him belong,
They are weak, but He is strong.

Refrain: Yes, Jesus loves me!
Yes, Jesus loves me!
Yes, Jesus loves me!
The Bible tells me so.

Jesus loves me! He who died
Heaven's gate to open wide;
He will wash away my sin,
Let His little child come in.

Jesus loves me! He will stay
Close beside me all the way;
Thou hast bled and died for me,
I will henceforth live for Thee.

HE'S GOT THE WHOLE WORLD

He's got the whole world in His hands, (repeat 3 more times)

He's got the wind and the rain in his hands, (repeat 2 more times)
He's got the whole world in His hands.

He's got the tiny little baby in His hands, (repeat 2 more times)
He's got the whole world in His hands.

He's got you and me, brother, in His hands,
He's got you and me, sister, in His hands,
He's got you and me, brother, in His hands,
He's got the whole world in His hands.

I HAVE DECIDED TO FOLLOW JESUS

I have decided to follow Jesus, (repeat 2 more times)
No turning back, no turning back.

The world behind me, the cross before me, (repeat 2 more times)
No turning back, no turning back.

Though none go with me, I still will follow, (repeat 2 more times)
No turning back, no turning back.

Will you decide now to follow Jesus? (repeat 2 more times)
No turning back, no turning back.

REJOICE IN THE LORD ALWAYS
(Makes a good four-part round)

Rejoice in the Lord always, again I say, rejoice! (Repeat 3 more times)

BLEST BE THE TIE THAT BINDS

Blest be the tie that binds
Our hearts in Christian love;
The fellowship of kindred minds
Is like to that above.

Before our Father's throne
We pour our ardent prayers;
Our fears, our hopes, our aims are one,
Our comforts and our cares.

We share our mutual woes,
Our mutual burdens bear;
And often for each other flows
The sympathizing tear.

When we asunder part,
It gives us inward pain;
But we shall still be joined in heart,
And hope to meet again.

OTHER IDEAL SONGS

Alleluia . . . .© 1972 Jerry Sinclair, Manna Music, Inc.
Be Glorified . . . .© 1978 Bob Kilpatrick Music
Bind Us Together . . . .© 1977 Maranatha! Music
Father, I Adore You . . . .© 1972 Maranatha! Music
Glorify Your Name . . . .© 1976 Maranatha! Music
He Is Lord . . . .© 1977 Marvin V. Frey
Pass it On . . . .© 1969 Communiquè Music
Seek Ye First the Kingdom of the Lord . . . .© 1972 Maranatha! Music
Spirit of the Living God . . . .© 1972 Sparrow Corp.

Appendix F

USEFUL TELEPHONE NUMBERS

"USA DIRECT" TELEPHONE COMPANIES

AT&T	(800) 321-0288
MCI	(800) 674-3000
Sprint	(800) 877-8000

U.S. GOVERNMENT AGENCIES

U.S. Passport Office - Boston	(617) 565-6990
U.S. Passport Office - Chicago	(312) 353-7155
U.S. Passport Office - Houston	(713) 653-3153
U.S. Passport Office - Los Angeles	(310) 235-7070
U.S. Passport Office - Miami	(305) 536-4681
U.S. Passport Office - New York	(202) 399-5290
U.S. Passport Office - Philadelphia	(215) 597-7480
U.S. Passport Office - San Francisco	(415) 744-4444
U.S. Passport Office - Seattle	(206) 220-7777
U.S. Passport Office - Washington, D. C.	(202) 647-0518
U.S. Department of Energy, Argonne Nat'l Laboratory	(708) 759-8901
U.S. Department of State, Overseas Citizens Services	(202) 647-5225
U.S. Consumer Information Center, Pueblo, CO.	(719) 948-3334
U.S. Customs Service	(202) 927-6724

TRAVEL INSURERS

Access America	(800) 284-8300
International SOS Assistance	(800) 523-8930
Mutual of Omaha	(800) 228-9792
Travel Guard International	(800) 782-5151
TravMed	(800) 732-5309

MISCELLANEOUS

Centers for Disease Control	(404) 639-2572
"Culturgrams"	(801) 378-6528
Int'l Association of Medical Assistance for Travelers	(716) 754-4883
Cirrus ATM card information	(800) 424-7787
PLUS ATM card information	(800) 491-1145
David C. Forward E-mail: DCForward@aol.com	(609) 988-1738

Appendix G

GUIDE TO SELECTED SHORT-TERM MISSION OPPORTUNITIES

This guide cross-refers the type of mission work in which readers are interested with the geographic areas they want to visit. Then look up the key code for the names and telephone contacts of those organizations that offer short-term mission opportunities in those areas. For example, if you want to do construction work in Africa, follow the matrix over to the "H," then on the following page the key will direct you to the Habitat for Humanity contact.

	USA/CANADA-RURAL	USA/CANADA-URBAN	AFRICA	ASIA	EUROPE/E. EUROPE	FORMER USSR	LATIN/SO. AMERICA
Aid to the Poor	K,W,G,Q	B,C*,W,G,K,Q,T	K	O,K,T	I,K,T	K	K
Children's Ministry	K,G,M*,Q,W,J	G,P,C*,W,J,K,Q,S,T	K,R	O,K,R,T	I,T	A,K	K,T,Z*
Church Planting	U,W,J,N,Q	W,J,Q,T,U	A,F,U,K,R	A,F,O,L,R,T	A,F,I,U,K,R,T	A,F,A,U,K	A,U,K
Community Development	K	C*,P,K,T	K	K,T	K,T	K	K
Construction	H,M*,K	H,K,C*,S	H,K,R	H	H,I	H	H,K
Hunger Relief	K	B,C*,K	E,K	E	E,K	K	K,E
Orphanage Care			K		I,K		
Evangelism & Fellowship	K,W,J,N,Q,T	B,C*,W,P,K,Q,S,T	A,F,U,K,R,T	A,F,O,L,R,T	A,F,K,I,R,T,U	A,F,U,A,K,R,T	A,U,K,R,T,Z*
Study/Teach Bible	K,W,J,Q	B,P,W,J,Q,T,U	U,K	T,U	J,T,U,	U,A,K,T	U,K,T
Teach/Provide Medical Care	W,K,D,V	W,U,K,D,V	D,K,V	I,D,K,V	K,U,D,V	D,U,K,V	U,D,K,Z*,V
Teaching Business Skills	W,K	W,K,T	T	T	T	T	
Teaching English	J	J,C*,K,T	K,R,T	L,O,E,R,T	R,T	K,T	K,T
Youth Ministry	W,G,M*,Q,T	P,C*,W,G, K,Q,T	K,T	K,T	I,T	K,T	K,T,Z*

See "Mission Organizations Key" on the next page for explanation & telephone numbers for above contacts.

MISSION ORGANIZATIONS KEY

An asterisk after the key code (ie: C*) indicates mission opportunities for student & youth groups.

KEY	ORGANIZATION	TELEPHONE	E-MAIL
A	Global Missions Fellowship	(972) 783-7476	gmf@computek.net
B	Olive Branch Mission	(773) 476-6200	
C*	Center for Student Missions	(714) 248-8200	csmhq@ix.netcom.com
D	Missionary Dentists	(206) 771-3241	chaliotis@aol.com
E	Food for the Hungry	(602) 998-3100	hunger@fh.org
F	Frontiers	(602) 834-1500	info@us.frontiers.org
G	Int'l Union of Gospel Missions	(816) 471-8020	sales@iugm.org
H	Habitat for Humanity	(912) 924-6935	www.habitat.org (Internet)
I	Int'l Children's Aid Foundation	(609) 988-1738	ICAF@aol.com
J	InterAct Ministries	(800) 258-3464	interactMn@aol.com
K	Presbyterian Church (USA)	(502) 569-5284	
L	Life Ministries	(800) 543-3678	71561.1373@Compuserve.com
M*	Mountain T.O.P	(615) 298-1575	onthemtop@aol.com
N	NAIM (N. American Indian Mission)	(604) 946-1227	102216.2755@Compuserve.com
O	OMF (Serve Asia)	(800) 422-5330	ctash@cproject.com
P	Urban Promise Ministries	(609) 964-5140	
Q	American Missionary Fellowship	(610) 527-4439	amfharstad@aol.com
R	TEAM The Evang. Alliance Mission	(800) 343-3144	team@teamworld.org
S	NY School of Urban Ministry	(718) 204-6471	nysum@aol.com
T	International Teams	(800) 323-0428	teaminfo@itusa.org
U	Gospel Missionary Union	(816) 734-8500	mhs:kreimer@gmu-kc
V	Medical Group Missions	(423) 844-1000	mgm@christian-doctors.com
W	World Impact	(213) 735-1137	info@worldimpact.org
Z*	Azusa Pacific University	(818) 812-3027	mccorkle@apu.edu

Moody Press, a ministry of Moody Bible Institute,
is designed for education, evangelization, and edification.
If we may assist you in knowing more about Christ
and the Christian life, please write us without obligation:
Moody Press, c/o MLM, Chicago, Illinois 60610.